Index

Thanks 7

Foreword 8

Chapter 1: Introduction 10

    1.1. The New Digital Era and the Challenges of Privacy 11

    1.2. Telecommunications and Paper in the Digital Age 11

    1.3. Global Connectivity and Increased Data Traffic 11

    1.4. The Value of Data in the Digital Age 12

    1.5. Privacy and Security: Core Challenges in the Telecommunications Sector 12

    1.6. Innovations in Data Security 13

    1.7. Social Responsibility and the Future of Telecommunications 14

    1.8. The Nature of Data and Exponential Growth 14

    1.9. The Exponential Growth of Data 15

    1.10. The Need for Protection and Privacy 15

    1.11. The Role of Data in the Development of New Technologies 16

    1.12. The Importance of a Data Protection Culture 17

    1.13. Privacy at Risk 17

    1.14. Risk in the Telecommunications Sector 18

    1.15. Consequences of Privacy Violations 18

    1.16. The Role of Companies and Regulators 19

    1.17. The New Culture of Privacy 20

    1.18. Main Data Protection Challenges 20

    1.19. The Impact of Global Regulations 21

    1.20. General Data Protection Regulation (GDPR) – European Union 21

    1.21. General Data Protection Law (LGPD) – Brazil 22

    1.22. California Consumer Privacy Act (CCPA) – United States 22

    1.23. Impact of Regulations on the Telecommunications Sector 23

    1.24. The Telecommunications Sector Under Regulation 24

    1.25. Data Collection and Storage 24

    1.26. Appointment of Data Protection Officers (DPO) 25

    1.27. Fines and Penalties 26

    1.28. Regulatory Complexity and Challenges for Multinational Enterprises 26

    1.29. Opportunity for Differentiation and Trust Building 27

Chapter 2: International Laws and Regulations 28

**DATA PROTECTION AND SECURITY IN THE TELECOMMUNICATIONS SECTOR
CHALLENGES AND SOLUTIONS IN THE DIGITAL AGE**

- 2.1 General Data Protection Regulation (GDPR) – European Union 28
  - GDPR Principles 28
  - Companies' Obligations under the GDPR 29
  - Case study: British Airways 29
- 2.2 General Data Protection Law (LGPD) – Brazil 30
  - Comparison with GDPR 30
  - Impact on the Telecommunications Sector 31
  - Practical Example: Vivo and Oi 32
- 2.3 CCPA (California Consumer Privacy Act) – EUA 33
  - Basic Principles 33
  - Impact on Telecom Operators 33
  - Case Study: Compliance and Innovation 34
- 2.4 Personal Data Protection Law in Angola (Law No. 22/11) 34
  - Local Obligations and Challenges 34
  - Case Studies 35

Chapter 3: Cybersecurity and Data Protection in the Telecommunications Sector 36
- 3.1 Cyber Risks and Threats in the Telecommunications Sector 36
  - 3.1.1 Phishing 36
  - 3.1.2 Ransomware 37
  - 3.1.3 DDoS (Distributed Denial of Service) 37
  - 3.1.4 Software and Hardware Vulnerabilities 38
  - 3.1.5 Insider Threats 38
  - 3.2 Security Measures to Protect Consumer Data 39
  - 3.2.1 Encryption 39
  - 3.2.2 Intrusion Monitoring and Detection 39
  - 3.2.3 Employee Training 40
  - 3.2.4 Security Updates and Patches 40
  - 3.2.5 Compliance with Data Protection Regulations 40
- 3.3 Importance of Compliance with Data Protection Regulations 41
  - 3.3.1 Consumer Protection 41
  - 3.3.2 Mitigation of Legal Risks 41
  - 3.3.3 Strengthening Brand Reputation 41
  - 3.3.4 International Business Facilitation 41
- 3.4 Conclusion 41

- 3.5 Security Measures for Data Protection 42
  - 3.5.1 Encryption 42
  - 3.5.2 Firewalls 42
  - 3.5.3 Zero-Trust Policies 43
  - 3.5.4 Network Segmentation 43
  - 3.5.5 Continuous Monitoring and Threat Detection 44
  - 3.5.6 Security Updates and Patches 44
  - 3.5.7 Employee Training 44
  - 3.5.8 Data Backup and Recovery 45
  - 3.5.9 Case Study: The Attack on TalkTalk 45
- 3.6 Compliance with Data Protection Regulations 46

Chapter 4: Emerging Technologies: 5G, IoT, and the New Frontier of Privacy 47
- 4.1 5G Networks and the Impact on Data Collection 47
- 4.2 Internet of Things (IoT) and Telecommunications 48
  - 4.2.1 IoT Challenges: 48
  - Case Study: Data Leaks in Medical Devices 49
- 5. Chapter Summary 49

Chapter 5: Advantages and Disadvantages of Strict Data Protection 50
- 5.1 Advantages 50
  - 5.1.1 Consumer Confidence 50
  - 5.1.2 Prevention of Fines and Sanctions 51
  - 5.1.3 Improvement of Internal Processes 51
  - 5.1.4 Competitive Advantage in Digital Markets 52
- 5.2 Disadvantages 52
  - 5.2.1 Cost of Implementation 52
  - 5.2.2 Regulatory Complexity 53
  - 5.2.3 Impact on Innovation 53
  - 5.2.4 Bureaucratization and Slowness in Processes 54
- 5.3 Chapter Summary 54

Chapter 6: Integration between Data Regulation and Telecommunications Expansion Policy 54
- 6.1 The Relationship between the Growth of Telecommunications and Data Protection 55
  - 6.1.1 Compliance Challenges in Expanding Networks 55
  - 6.1.2 Responsible Innovation and Data Protection 56
  - 6.1.3 Benefits of Compliance in Technological Expansion 56

DATA PROTECTION AND SECURITY IN THE TELECOMMUNICATIONS SECTOR CHALLENGES AND SOLUTIONS IN THE DIGITAL AGE

- 6.2 The Importance of Public-Private Partnerships 57
  - 6.2.1 Effective Policy Development 57
  - 6.2.2 Education and Awareness 57
  - 6.2.3 Development of Secure Technologies 58
  - 6.2.4 Rapid Incident Responses 58
- 6.3 Chapter Summary 58

Chapter 7: Conclusions and Recommendations 59
- 7.1 The Future of Data Protection in the Telecommunications Industry 59
  - Adaptation of Regulations 60
  - Education and Awareness 61
- 7.2 Practical Recommendations for Telecommunications Companies 62
  - Chapter Summary 63
- 7.2 Practical Recommendations for Telecommunications Companies 63
  - Steps to Implement Compliance Policies 63
  - Best Practices to Ensure Data Security and Privacy 65
- Chapter Summary 67

Chapter 8: Case Studies and Examples 68
- Case 1: GDPR Implementation in European Union Companies 68
  - Challenges 69
  - Solution 69
  - Results 70
- Case 2: Adjustments to the LGPD in Brazil 70
  - Context 70
  - Challenges 70
  - Solution 71
  - Results 71
- Case 3: CCPA's Impact on U.S. Carriers 71
  - Context 72
  - Challenges 72
  - Solution 72
  - Results 73
- Example 4: Sonangol and Unitel's compliance with Angola's Data Protection Law 73
  - Context 73
  - Challenges 73

DATA PROTECTION AND SECURITY IN THE TELECOMMUNICATIONS SECTOR
CHALLENGES AND SOLUTIONS IN THE DIGITAL AGE

- Solution 74
- Results 74
- Chapter Summary 75
- Conclusion: The Integration Between Data Protection and Telecommunications Expansion 76
  - The Central Role of Telecommunications in the 21st Century 76
  - Topics Addressed: Challenges and Solutions 76
  - Personal and Professional Application: Opportunities and Responsibilities 77
  - Professional Application 78
  - Personal Application 78
  - The Future of Telecommunications and Data Protection 79
- Final Thoughts 79

DATA PROTECTION AND SECURITY IN THE TELECOMMUNICATIONS SECTOR
CHALLENGES AND SOLUTIONS IN THE DIGITAL AGE

DATA PROTECTION AND SECURITY IN THE TELECOMMUNICATIONS SECTOR

CHALLENGES AND SOLUTIONS IN THE DIGITAL AGE

Thanks

The journey of writing this book was marked by challenges, discoveries, and a deep sense of learning and gratitude. Getting to this point would not have been possible without the support, affection and collaboration of special people who have been by my side, offering encouragement, advice and inspiration.

First of all, I would like to express my sincere gratitude to my family, who, with unconditional love and patience, supported me every step of the way. The affection and support of each one of you were fundamental for me to maintain the focus and determination necessary to complete this project.

To Eng. Diogo José de Carvalho, CEO and Miguel Ferreira of Infrasat Telecomunicações, S.A., who have always motivated me and believed in my potential, I thank you for being present, even in the most difficult times. His words of encouragement were essential for me to never give up, even in the face of obstacles.

A special thanks goes to Ana de Almeida, whose collaboration was essential for the realization of this book. His vision, competence and dedication exceeded all expectations. Without his thorough assistance and tireless commitment, this project would not have reached the depth and quality that it has. Your input has truly been invaluable, and I am deeply grateful to have had the privilege of working alongside you.

To all those who, in some way, were involved in the creation of this book, thank you very much. Their influences, direct or indirect, are part of this work, and it is, in many ways, a reflection of the valuable connections I have built along this journey.

This book is the result of a collective effort, and to everyone who was part of this path, I leave here my most sincere gratitude.

With appreciation and respect,

Manuel Gomes

Foreword

The digital age has brought with it a revolution in terms of how personal data is collected, stored, and used. We live in a world where information has become one of the most valuable assets, and its protection is more critical than ever.

In this new context, companies, especially in the telecommunications sector, deal daily with large volumes of data that need to be safeguarded effectively.

Not only do these organizations store personal information, but they also have an ethical and legal duty to ensure the privacy and security of their customers' data.

The exponential increase in connectivity and the use of mobile devices has generated a constant flow of data, ranging from basic information such as names and addresses to sensitive data such as health and financial information.

In this scenario, consumer trust has become an essential aspect for the success of any telecommunications company.

Consumers are increasingly aware of their rights regarding privacy and expect companies to protect their personal data in a robust and transparent manner.

Not only does this translate into stricter regulations, such as the General Data Protection Regulation (GDPR) in the European Union, but also a growing need to adopt compliance practices that ensure data security.

This book not only explores the regulations that shape this landscape, but also offers a practical look at compliance and security policies, with real-world cases that demonstrate the evolution and challenges faced by companies around the world.

Throughout the chapters, we look at how different jurisdictions implement data protection laws and how these legislations impact the operations of telecommunications companies.

The case studies presented reflect the diversity of situations that arise at the intersection of technology and regulation, and how companies can learn from each other when addressing these common challenges.

In addition, this book seeks to offer practical recommendations that can be used by professionals in the field, from telecommunications managers to compliance and information security officers.

We hope that the guidance presented here will help companies develop and implement effective data protection policies that not only meet legal requirements, but also promote a culture of privacy and security within organizations.

I invite all readers to delve deeper into the contents covered in this book and to reflect on how they can apply these concepts in their own professional practices.

We believe that by promoting a deeper understanding of data protection in the telecommunications industry, we can contribute to a safer and more ethical future in the management of personal information.

I hope this book serves as a useful tool for professionals navigating the complex world of data protection and for those seeking to understand how telecommunications, one of the most crucial sectors of the global economy, are adjusting to this new paradigm.

Manuel Gomes

Author

DATA PROTECTION AND SECURITY IN THE TELECOMMUNICATIONS SECTOR
CHALLENGES AND SOLUTIONS IN THE DIGITAL AGE

Chapter 1: Introduction

The digital age has brought a profound transformation to society, changing the way we connect, interact, and use technologies.

At the center of this new scenario is data, which has come to be considered the "new oil", boosting economies and enabling unprecedented technological innovations.

However, with the exponential increase in the collection and use of personal information, critical challenges related to data privacy and security arise.

This book comprehensively examines the impacts of this new digital era, with an emphasis on the telecommunications sector and the essential role it plays in global connectivity.

Through telecommunications networks, a continuous flow of data is generated and shared, which puts operators at the center of an increasingly urgent debate on data protection and privacy.

In addition to exploring the opportunities for innovation generated by the use of data, this book looks at the risks and responsibilities of companies in complying with global regulations.

Regulations such as the General Data Protection Regulation (GDPR) in the European Union, the General Data Protection Law (LGPD) in Brazil, and the California Consumer Privacy Act (CCPA) in the United States have created new requirements that profoundly shape the way companies handle consumer data.

The implications of these laws are not limited to legal issues; They impact consumer confidence, corporate reputation, and competitiveness in the global marketplace.

This book seeks not only to map the main challenges that companies face in data management and protection, but also to highlight how these regulations can be a strategic opportunity for organizations that adopt a proactive stance.

Implementing a strong and ethical data protection culture can become a competitive differentiator, attracting consumers who are increasingly concerned about their privacy.

Through a detailed analysis of the technical, legal, and strategic aspects of data protection, this book serves as an essential guide for industry professionals, academics, and anyone interested in understanding the future of privacy in the digital age.

**DATA PROTECTION AND SECURITY IN THE TELECOMMUNICATIONS SECTOR
CHALLENGES AND SOLUTIONS IN THE DIGITAL AGE**

1.1. The New Digital Era and the Challenges of Privacy

The digital age, characterized by the rapid expansion of information and communication technology, has profoundly transformed the ways we live, work, and interact.

With the massive integration of internet-connected devices and the digitization of personal and business data, privacy has become a central topic of concern.

The new digital era has brought incredible opportunities, such as automation, big data analytics, the Internet of Things (IoT), and artificial intelligence (AI), but it has also opened doors to new vulnerabilities.

The main challenge of digital privacy lies in how data is collected, stored and used. Tech companies, governments, and organizations now have access to unprecedented amounts of personal information, which raises ethical and legal questions about the use of this data.

In addition, hacker intrusion and the exposure of sensitive information are constant concerns. Privacy in the digital age, therefore, requires a multi-dimensional approach that encompasses legal regulations, protection technology, and the awareness of individuals about the protection of their own data.

1.2. Telecommunications and Paper in the Digital Age

The telecommunications sector is one of the pillars of the digital age. By providing the infrastructures of communication networks, such as broadband internet, 4G/5G mobile networks, and satellite connections, this sector enables global connectivity, enabling the interconnection of devices and the flow of data that feed the digital economy.

Telecommunications facilitate real-time information sharing, support the growth of emerging technologies, and enable the development of new digital industries.

In addition to its basic function of connecting people and devices, telecommunications play a strategic role in digital transformation initiatives, such as smart cities and the development of industrial internet networks.

With the advancement of 5G, the industry is leading the technological revolution, enabling minimal latency and unprecedented data transmission speed.

However, this innovation also brings challenges, such as increased vulnerability to digital espionage, cyberattacks, and data misuse.

1.3. Global Connectivity and Increased Data Traffic

Global connectivity has been growing exponentially with the proliferation of smartphones, connected devices, and the expansion of the internet to remote areas.

The Internet of Things (IoT), which connects devices such as sensors, cameras, and home appliances to the internet, has boosted data traffic significantly. In 2020, it was estimated that more than 50 billion devices were connected to the internet, a number that continues to grow.

This increase in connectivity generated an explosion in the volume of data trafficked in telecommunications networks. Global mobile data traffic, for example, is growing at a compound annual rate of more than 30 percent, Cisco reports, with video and streaming services accounting for the majority of that traffic.

As more devices are connected and more data is transmitted, questions arise related to network capacity, data security, and the need to innovate in telecommunications infrastructures to support this growth.

1.4. The Value of Data in the Digital Age

In the digital age, data is one of the most valuable assets, often compared to oil due to its economic and strategic potential. They are the raw material that powers a vast array of emerging technologies, such as artificial intelligence (AI), machine learning, and big data analytics.

With data, companies can generate deep insights into consumer behavior, improve operational efficiency, personalize experiences, and even accurately predict future trends.

The value of data is not only limited to its volume, but also to its ability to be transformed into useful information through analysis processes.

With the ability to identify patterns and correlate information, data has the power to transform entire industries, from digital marketing to healthcare, transportation, and manufacturing.

However, as the value of data grows, so does the responsibility of companies to ensure that this information is collected and used ethically, securely, and in compliance with privacy regulations.

1.5. Privacy and Security: Core Challenges in the Telecommunications Sector

The telecommunications sector, as a primary vehicle for large-scale data transmission, faces unique challenges in relation to privacy and security.

Telecommunications networks are the main means by which personal and business data travel, which makes them preferred targets for cyberattacks and espionage.

In addition, with the advent of technologies such as 5G, IoT, and cloud computing, the attack surface has expanded, increasing the complexity of ensuring data security at every stage of its transmission.

One of the biggest challenges is ensuring that user data remains protected from unauthorized access and that critical infrastructure is proof against cyberattacks.

Telecommunications companies need to invest heavily in encryption technologies, intrusion detection systems, and robust security protocols to mitigate these risks.

However, in addition to technical challenges, the industry also faces regulatory pressures, with governments around the world imposing new data protection and privacy requirements.

Compliance with these regulations requires a delicate balance between the need for technological innovation and meeting stringent safety standards.

This is the first part with five detailed topics. If everything is in order, I can continue with the next topics or make any adjustments you need.

1.6. Innovations in Data Security

With the increased threat of cyberattacks and data breaches, security innovations have become crucial for protecting sensitive information.

Advanced encryption, multi-factor authentication (MFA), and artificial intelligence technologies are at the forefront of ensuring data security in increasingly complex digital environments.

Modern encryption, which transforms data into unreadable codes to ensure privacy during transmission and storage, is one of the pillars of digital security.

In addition, multi-factor authentication, which requires multiple forms of verification (e.g., passwords and biometric recognition), makes it much more difficult for attackers to gain unauthorized access to systems or networks.

Artificial intelligence (AI) also plays a growing role in data security. AI-based systems are able to detect anomalies in network traffic, identifying patterns of behavior that can signal intrusion attempts or malicious activity.

Tools such as blockchain, which offer an immutable record of transactions, are also being explored to increase security in financial systems and other industries.

In addition to these technologies, cloud-centric security solutions are also gaining prominence. With the migration of data and services to the cloud, cloud-based security solutions offer continuous monitoring, automated threat responses, and greater scalability for large volumes of data.

1.7. Social Responsibility and the Future of Telecommunications

Telecommunications play a key role not only as enablers of global connectivity, but also as agents of social and economic transformation.

Companies in the sector must take on a growing social responsibility, which goes beyond simply providing connectivity services. They need to ensure that their technological expansion is inclusive, accessible, and respects consumers' privacy rights.

In the future of telecommunications, issues such as digital inclusion, environmental sustainability, and ethical privacy practices will be at the center of discussions.

Social responsibility includes ensuring that telecommunications networks are available in rural areas and in hard-to-reach regions, promoting digital inclusion.

In addition, the sector has a responsibility to minimize the environmental impact associated with the installation of infrastructure, such as antennas and submarine cables, and energy consumption.

Another key point in the future of telecommunications will be the commitment to user privacy.

The ethical use of personal data should be a priority, and companies that adopt a responsible and transparent stance towards data collection and use will be in a better position to earn the public's trust and thrive in an increasingly competitive market.

1.8. The Nature of Data and Exponential Growth

Data, in its most basic form, is raw information generated from human interactions and technological processes. However, in the digital age, this data is more than just records; They have become one of the most valuable assets for businesses and organizations.

The nature of data is varied, ranging from structured data (such as tables and records) to unstructured data (such as videos, images, and text), all of which are generated in unprecedented volumes.

The exponential growth of data is a reflection of the global increase in the use of digital technologies. Social networks, connected devices, streaming services, e-commerce, and even online financial transactions generate trillions of bytes of data daily.

The concept of "big data" emerged precisely to describe the immense volume and complexity of the data generated, which requires sophisticated technological solutions to be stored, processed and analyzed.

This growth also creates new challenges, such as the need for more efficient data storage infrastructures, new ways to process large volumes of information, and, of course, the protection of this data from inappropriate use or leakage.

1.9. The Exponential Growth of Data

The exponential growth of data stems from a variety of sources, including connected devices, social media platforms, and the widespread use of cloud-based services.

The Internet of Things (IoT), which connects everything from home appliances to cars and industrial sensors, is one of the main drivers of this data increase.

Each connected device collects and transmits information in real time, contributing to the immense volume of data circulating globally.

The expansion of technologies such as 5G also facilitates the increase in data traffic. With higher speeds and greater capacity of connected devices, 5G networks are key to supporting the growth of IoT and other technologies that require large volumes of data transmission.

In addition, the exponential growth of data is closely linked to digital transformation in industries such as healthcare, finance, and education, where the digitization of records and the automation of processes generate enormous amounts of information that need to be managed and protected.

This increase brings technical challenges, such as the need for greater storage and processing capacity, as well as privacy and security challenges, as a higher volume of data implies greater risks.

1.10. The Need for Protection and Privacy

The need for protection and privacy has become a central concern amid the explosion of digital data. The massive amount of information circulating on the internet, much of it of a personal or sensitive nature, makes users vulnerable to privacy breaches, identity theft, and misuse of their data.

Thus, the protection of privacy is no longer just a matter of individual security, but a fundamental right that needs to be ensured.

In addition, with the proliferation of cyberattacks and data leaks, the need to protect personal information has never been more urgent.

Governments and regulatory bodies around the world are adopting stringent laws and regulations to ensure that companies act responsibly in their handling of personal data.

The European Union's General Data Protection Regulation (GDPR) and the General Data Protection Law (LGPD) in Brazil are examples of how legislation is adapting to this new reality, imposing severe penalties for privacy violations.

Organizations need to invest in robust security solutions, such as encryption, restricted access policies, continuous network monitoring, and compliance training for their employees, to ensure they are complying with legal requirements and, most importantly, protecting their customers' and users' data. Consumer trust in a company is closely tied to its ability to protect privacy.

1.11. The Role of Data in the Development of New Technologies

Data is the fuel that drives most new technologies. Innovations such as artificial intelligence (AI), machine learning, automation, and predictive analytics rely on large volumes of data to function and continuously improve.

AI, for example, uses historical and real-time data to learn and make more accurate and efficient decisions, something that would be impossible without the continuous collection and analysis of information.

In industries such as healthcare, data is revolutionizing precision medicine, where treatments are personalized based on each patient's genetic profile and medical history.

In industry, data is transforming manufacturing through intelligent automation, optimizing processes, and reducing waste. Even in the field of public security, data is helping to predict and prevent crimes with the use of predictive algorithms.

Therefore, the role of data in the development of new technologies cannot be underestimated. However, the responsible access and use of this data is a key point, since without proper protection, the misuse of personal information can compromise trust in emerging technologies.

1.12. The Importance of a Data Protection Culture

A culture of data protection within organizations is essential to ensure the privacy and security of sensitive information.

It's not enough to just implement advanced security technologies; It is necessary that all members of an organization, from senior management to operational employees, are committed to data protection.

The culture of data protection involves the adoption of clear and effective information handling policies, as well as the promotion of an ongoing awareness of security best practices.

Regular training on privacy, the proper use of security tools, and compliance with data protection regulations are essential to ensure that all levels of the organization understand their responsibilities.

Companies that foster a strong culture of data protection also build trust with their customers and partners. By demonstrating a commitment to privacy and security, organizations not only protect their operations but also stand out in an increasingly competitive market where consumers are increasingly concerned about the security of their personal information.

1.13. Privacy at Risk

Privacy risk has become a global concern due to the exponential growth of digital data and the complexity of the systems that handle it.

Devices connected to the internet, social networks, and online services constantly collect data, often without the full knowledge or consent of users.

This vast volume of data creates opportunities for businesses and governments, but it also exposes individuals to potential privacy breaches.

Additionally, cyberattacks such as identity theft, phishing, and ransomware are becoming increasingly sophisticated, threatening the integrity of personal and corporate data.

Excessive data collection, often done by technology platforms without a clear or explicit purpose, increases the risk of misuse of information.

Because of this, the concept of "privacy by design" is gaining traction, requiring data protection to be incorporated from the beginning into the development of technologies and services.

Privacy risks are also linked to some companies' lack of transparency about how data is used. This highlights the importance of robust regulations and the need for ongoing oversight to protect citizens' privacy rights.

1.14. Risk in the Telecommunications Sector

The telecommunications sector is especially vulnerable to security and privacy risks due to its central position in the digital infrastructure.

Telecommunications companies handle vast amounts of user data, including calls, text messages, internet browsing data, and geolocation, making them attractive targets for hackers and cybercriminals.

One of the main risks in the sector is the attack on telecommunications networks for espionage or theft of confidential information. The advent of 5G, which allows billions of devices to connect to the internet at high speeds, amplifies these risks, as it creates a much larger attack surface for potential attackers.

Another significant risk is interference from state actors or organized groups that can compromise the security of telecommunications networks through espionage or sabotage.

The ability to ensure that telecommunications networks are secure and resilient against cyberattacks is one of the most pressing challenges faced by companies in this sector.

1.15. Consequences of Privacy Violations

Privacy violations can have devastating consequences for individuals and organizations alike. At the individual level, the exposure of personal data can lead to identity theft, financial fraud, and other crimes, causing significant financial and emotional damage to victims. In more serious cases, such as the exposure of medical data or sensitive personal information, the impact can be irreparable.

For businesses, privacy breaches have financial, reputational, and legal consequences. Millionaire fines can be imposed by regulatory authorities, as in the case of the General Data Protection Regulation (GDPR) in the European Union, which can apply penalties of up to 4% of the company's annual global revenue. In addition to financial penalties, businesses can also experience a loss of trust from their customers, resulting in dropped business and brand damage.

In addition, the exposure of confidential information can harm business negotiations, partnerships, and even compromise national security, especially in sectors such as telecommunications and defense. The long-term consequences of a privacy breach, therefore, can be severe and, in some cases, irreversible.

1.16. The Role of Companies and Regulators

The role of companies and regulators in data protection and privacy is complementary but distinct.

Companies have a responsibility to implement secure data collection, storage, and handling practices, ensuring that their users' information is protected from unauthorized access and misuse.

This includes investing in security technologies, training employees, and adopting policies to comply with data protection laws.

On the other hand, regulators have the function of establishing clear and enforceable guidelines to protect citizens' privacy, as well as monitoring and enforcing these regulations.

The creation of legal frameworks, such as the GDPR in the European Union and the General Data Protection Law (LGPD) in Brazil, demonstrates the growing commitment of governments to protecting privacy in the digital age.

These regulations impose strict requirements for companies to inform and obtain consent from users before collecting data, in addition to forcing them to report privacy violations within a certain timeframe.

Collaboration between businesses and regulators is essential to creating a secure and reliable digital environment. Together, they can ensure that individuals' privacy rights are respected while encouraging technological innovation and economic growth.

1.17. The New Culture of Privacy

The new privacy culture is characterized by a growing focus on data protection as a fundamental right and on the responsibility of companies to respect this right.

Consumers are increasingly aware of the value of their data and demand greater transparency and control over how their information is used.

This cultural movement is being driven not only by legislation such as GDPR, LGPD, and CCPA, but also by a shift in consumer expectations.

Companies that take a proactive stance on privacy, offering tools to control data and acting transparently, are gaining the trust of customers and differentiating themselves in an increasingly competitive market.

In addition, privacy culture is becoming a point of differentiation for companies that use data protection as a competitive advantage.

Those who invest in robust privacy and security practices are positioning their brands as trustworthy and ethical, which can be a deciding factor for consumers when choosing products and services.

1.18. Main Data Protection Challenges

The challenges of data protection are numerous and range from technological issues to regulatory and organizational aspects.

Among the main challenges faced by companies in the digital age is the balance between the effective use of data and ensuring privacy.

Companies need to leverage data to drive innovation and create personalized experiences for customers, but they must do so within the bounds of regulations and privacy rights.

Another major challenge is the rapid evolution of cyber threats. As new technologies emerge, so do new types of attacks, such as sophisticated phishing, ransomware, and security breaches involving connected devices (IoT).

The growing volume of data also makes it difficult to implement security solutions at scale, especially for companies operating globally.

Regulatory compliance is another significant hurdle. Businesses need to comply with different laws and regulations in different jurisdictions, which can be complex and costly.

In addition, training employees to ensure that everyone understands the importance of privacy and data protection is an ongoing and essential task, but not always easy to implement effectively.

1.19. The Impact of Global Regulations

Global data protection regulations, such as GDPR in the European Union, LGPD in Brazil, and CCPA in the United States, have had a profound impact on the way companies handle data.

They force organizations to rethink their information collection, storage, and processing practices, imposing new requirements for transparency, consent, and data governance.

These regulations not only introduce new legal requirements, but also change the way consumers interact with businesses.

Mandatory informed consent and the ability for users to request the deletion of their data strengthen individual rights over privacy.

For companies, this can mean increased responsibility and the need to adopt technological tools to ensure compliance.

The financial impact is also significant. Fines imposed for non-compliance can be extremely high, representing up to 4% of a company's global annual turnover, in the case of GDPR.

In addition, regulations force companies to invest in security infrastructure, employee training, and specialized teams, such as data protection officers (DPOs), which can increase operating costs.

1.20. General Data Protection Regulation (GDPR) – European Union

The European Union's General Data Protection Regulation (GDPR), implemented in May 2018, is one of the strictest and most comprehensive privacy regulations in the world.

It is designed to protect the personal data of European citizens and to give them more control over how their information is used.

The GDPR does not only apply to companies based in the European Union, but to any organization that processes data of EU citizens, regardless of where the company is located.

Among the main aspects of the GDPR are the requirement for explicit consent from users for the use of their data, the right to request the deletion of data ("right to be forgotten"), the obligation to quickly notify authorities of security breaches, and the imposition of designating a data protection officer (DPO) to oversee compliance with the rules.

The impact of the GDPR has been global, with many companies outside of Europe adopting similar standards to avoid severe fines and to demonstrate a commitment to privacy. The regulation also served as a model for later legislation, such as the LGPD in Brazil and the CCPA in the United States.

1.21. General Data Protection Law (LGPD) – Brazil

The General Data Protection Law (LGPD), which came into force in Brazil in September 2020, was created to ensure the protection of the personal data of Brazilian citizens and to standardize privacy practices throughout the country.

Inspired by the European GDPR, the LGPD establishes rules for the collection, processing, and storage of personal data, giving individuals greater power over their own information.

Among the rights guaranteed by the LGPD are the right to know what data is being collected, the right to request the correction or deletion of data, and the right to revoke consent to the use of your information.

Companies are also required to adopt technical and organizational measures to protect data, and violations can result in heavy fines, which reach 2% of annual gross revenue, with a limit of 50 million reais per violation.

The creation of the National Data Protection Authority (ANPD) was also an important milestone in the application of the LGPD, as this entity is responsible for supervising and ensuring compliance with the rules.

Like the GDPR, the LGPD does not only affect Brazilian companies, but any organization that processes data of Brazilian citizens, which makes it a regulation with a global impact.

1.22. California Consumer Privacy Act (CCPA) – United States

The California Consumer Privacy Act (CCPA), which went into effect in 2020, is one of the most comprehensive data protection laws in the United States.

Focused on strengthening the privacy rights of consumers in California, the CCPA sets new standards for how companies should handle the personal data of the state's residents.

Under the CCPA, consumers have the right to know what data is being collected, why it is being collected, and with whom it is being shared.

They can also request the deletion of their data and opt out of having their personal information sold to third parties.

Unlike GDPR, which requires prior consent, CCPA focuses more on providing consumers with the ability to control the use of their data after collection.

The impact of the CCPA goes beyond California, as many companies choose to adopt its standards throughout the U.S., to avoid the complexity of dealing with different state regulations.

The CCPA has also paved the way for debates about a possible federal data protection law in the United States, highlighting the growing importance of privacy in American society.

1.23. Impact of Regulations on the Telecommunications Sector

Data protection regulations such as GDPR, LGPD, and CCPA have a significant impact on the telecommunications industry, which deals with massive volumes of personal data on a daily basis.

Telecommunications companies are required to ensure that they are compliant with regulations, which requires substantial investments in security, training, and technology.

The telecommunications sector, due to its critical nature, is particularly under scrutiny from regulators.

Companies need to implement robust policies to ensure that user information, such as location data, calls, and internet browsing, is protected.

Any privacy violation can result in severe penalties, as well as cause significant damage to the company's reputation.

Another impact of the regulations is the requirement for rapid notification in case of security breaches.

This forces telecom operators to maintain constant vigilance over their networks and to be transparent with consumers about potential risks.

In addition, regulations encourage the development of more advanced security solutions to meet compliance demands and better protect user data.

1.24. The Telecommunications Sector Under Regulation

The telecommunications sector is one of the most regulated in terms of data protection, due to the sensitivity and volume of information that companies in this sector manage.

Global regulation requires these organizations to adopt strict measures to protect personal data and ensure user privacy.

Telecom operators manage a wide range of data, such as call logs, text messages, geolocation data, and internet traffic, which makes them priority targets for cyberattacks.

In addition to data protection, telecommunications companies also need to comply with industry-specific regulations, which vary by jurisdiction, to ensure the security of communication networks.

This includes obligations to keep communications records for a certain period of time, cooperation with authorities for legal investigations, and compliance with regulations related to net neutrality and spectrum use.

The regulations aim to ensure that companies in the telecommunications sector have transparent practices regarding the collection and use of data, which include explicit consent from users, auditing procedures, and prompt notifications in the event of a data breach.

Compliance with these standards is vital not only to avoid hefty fines, but also to preserve consumer trust and the integrity of the communication infrastructure.

1.25. Data Collection and Storage

Data collection and storage are critical processes that, in the digital age, pose considerable challenges and responsibilities for businesses, especially in the telecommunications sector.

These processes involve capturing large volumes of information about users, such as their media consumption habits, location, and daily communications, which is then stored on servers and datacenters.

One of the biggest challenges with respect to data collection is to ensure that this activity takes place in a transparent and ethical manner, based on the consent of individuals.

Regulations such as GDPR and LGPD impose the need for companies to clearly explain the reason for collection, how the data will be used, and how long it will be retained.

Companies that fail to adhere to these standards can be fined and suffer damage to their reputation.

In data storage, the main concern is security. Ensuring that the data collected is stored securely, protected by encryption, and that access is limited to authorized people, is essential to prevent breaches and cyberattacks.

Proper data lifecycle management, including secure deletion when data is no longer needed, is also a critical requirement in various global regulations.

1.26. Appointment of Data Protection Officers (DPO)

The appointment of a Data Protection Officer (DPO) is a central requirement in data protection regulations, such as the GDPR and LGPD.

The DPO is responsible for ensuring that the organization is compliant with data protection laws and for acting as a point of contact between the company and regulatory authorities.

The duties of a DPO include overseeing the company's privacy and security policies, conducting regular audits, assessing security risks, and advising senior management on data protection best practices.

In addition, the DPO must ensure that the rights of individuals, such as access to and correction of their data, are respected and that there is transparency in all processes involving personal data.

The appointment of a DPO is particularly important in large companies that process large volumes of data or that handle sensitive information.

Additionally, the role of the DPO has gained importance as the complexity of global regulations increases, requiring companies to have in-house experts capable of navigating this complex regulatory environment.

1.27. Fines and Penalties

The fines and penalties associated with violating data protection regulations can be extremely severe, and are one of the main incentive mechanisms for companies to comply with the rules.

Under GDPR, for example, penalties can reach up to €20 million or 4% of the company's global annual turnover, whichever is greater.

This proportionate approach aims to ensure that large corporations do not consider fines as mere operational costs and take data protection seriously.

In Brazil, the LGPD also imposes fines that can reach 2% of the company's gross revenue, limited to 50 million reais per violation.

In the United States, the CCPA also has mechanisms in place to penalize companies that disrespect consumers' privacy rights, although the fines are more directly proportional to the number of privacy incidents.

In addition to financial penalties, companies may face other types of sanctions, such as temporarily suspending their activities or blocking certain services.

The consequences of a privacy breach can also include civil lawsuits, in which affected individuals seek compensation for damages.

The penalties are not restricted to the financial side alone: the loss of customer trust can cause irreparable damage to the brand's reputation, leading to loss of business in the long run.

1.28. Regulatory Complexity and Challenges for Multinational Enterprises

For multinational companies, compliance with data protection regulations is particularly challenging due to the complexity and diversity of laws in different countries and regions.

Each jurisdiction may have its own specific rules and requirements regarding data collection, storage, processing, and transfer, which requires strict management to ensure that the company is compliant with all of them.

For example, a company operating in Europe needs to follow the GDPR, while in Brazil it must comply with the LGPD, and in the United States, with legislation such as the CCPA.

Additionally, some jurisdictions impose additional restrictions on the transfer of data outside of their borders, requiring companies to ensure that data is transferred securely and in accordance with local regulations.

This scenario creates the need for a global approach to data governance, but it also requires adapting to local specificities.

Companies often need to maintain legal and compliance teams in multiple regions to ensure they are complying with all relevant regulations.

The operational cost and complexity of this task is significant, and errors in the interpretation or application of regulations can result in hefty fines and penalties.

1.29. Opportunity for Differentiation and Trust Building

Despite the challenges that data protection regulations impose, they also offer a unique opportunity for companies to differentiate themselves in the market.

By taking a proactive approach to privacy and security, organizations can build a reputation for trust and accountability, which translates into a competitive advantage.

Consumers are increasingly concerned about how their data is handled and tend to value companies that demonstrate a serious commitment to protecting their information.

Companies that go beyond the minimum required by regulations, implementing better security and privacy practices, are more likely to attract and retain customers.

Transparency in data collection and use practices, along with clear and open communication about privacy issues, can create a stronger relationship with consumers based on mutual trust.

In addition, compliance with stringent regulations can be seen as a seal of quality in highly competitive markets.

Organizations that excel in terms of data protection not only avoid fines, but also create a differentiator that can be used in marketing strategies to attract customers who value privacy.

Therefore, privacy and data protection regulations offer both challenges and opportunities for modern businesses.

Chapter 2: International Laws and Regulations

This chapter explores the main data protection legislations in the world and how they directly impact the telecommunications sector.

2.1 General Data Protection Regulation (GDPR) – European Union

The General Data Protection Regulation (GDPR), implemented in May 2018, represents a significant milestone in privacy and data protection legislation in the European Union (EU).

The GDPR is designed to strengthen and unify data protection for all individuals within the EU, as well as to address the export of personal data outside the EU.

The regulation applies to all companies that process data of individuals in the EU, regardless of where those companies are located.

GDPR Principles

The GDPR is based on fundamental principles that guide the processing of personal data. These principles are essential to ensure that personal information is treated ethically and transparently:

1. Explicit Consent: Personal data can only be processed if there is explicit consent on the part of the holder. This means that organizations must be clear about how and why data is being collected and utilized.

2. Specific Purpose: Data must be collected for legitimate and specific purposes and must not be processed in a manner that is incompatible with those purposes. This ensures that the data is not misused.

3. Data Minimization: Only data that is necessary for the specific purpose should be collected. This means that businesses should avoid over-gathering information by sticking to what they actually need.

4. Integrity and Confidentiality: Organizations must ensure that personal data is treated in a manner that ensures its security, including protection against unauthorized or unlawful processing and against accidental loss, destruction, or damage.

5. Accountability and Transparency: Companies are responsible for ensuring compliance with the GDPR and must be able to demonstrate this compliance. This includes keeping records of processing activities and providing clear information about how data is handled.

Companies' Obligations under the GDPR

To ensure compliance with GDPR principles, companies have several obligations:

1. Appointing a Data Protection Officer (DPO): Organizations that process large volumes of personal data or sensitive data must appoint a DPO who is responsible for monitoring compliance with the GDPR, acting as a point of contact for data subjects, and cooperating with data protection authorities.

2. Notification of Data Breaches: Companies must notify the competent data protection authority and data subjects of any personal data breach within 72 hours of detection, unless the breach does not pose a risk to the rights and freedoms of individuals.

3. Exercising Data Subject Rights: The GDPR guarantees data subjects a range of rights, including the right to access their personal data, the right to rectification, the right to erasure (right to be forgotten), the right to data portability, and the right to object to processing. Companies must implement processes to enable holders to exercise these rights efficiently.

Case study: British Airways

One of the most emblematic examples of GDPR enforcement occurred with British Airways, which was fined £183 million in July 2019 for a data breach that affected approximately 500,000 customers.

The breach occurred due to a security flaw in its website, which allowed hackers to access personal and financial information of customers who were making reservations online.

This case highlighted not only the severity of sanctions under the GDPR but also the importance of implementing robust security measures to protect personal data.

The £183 million fine was one of the largest ever imposed under the regulation, highlighting the responsibility of companies to ensure data security and the need to take data protection seriously in an increasingly digital world.

In addition, the case of British Airways serves as a warning to other companies about the consequences of non-compliance with the GDPR.

It reinforces the need to invest in cybersecurity infrastructure and proper compliance practices to avoid financial penalties and reputational damage.

2.2 General Data Protection Law (LGPD) – Brazil

The General Data Protection Law (LGPD), sanctioned in 2018 and in force since September 2020, is the Brazilian legislation that regulates the collection, storage, processing, and sharing of personal data in the national territory.

Inspired by the European Union's GDPR, the LGPD was a response to the growing need to protect the rights of individuals in the digital world and represents a milestone for companies, especially those in the telecommunications sector, which process large volumes of personal data on a daily basis.

Comparison with GDPR

The LGPD shares several fundamental principles with the European Union's General Data Protection Regulation (GDPR), but with some particularities adapted to the Brazilian context:

1. Consent and Transparency: Like the GDPR, the LGPD requires consent to be informed, explicit, and freely provided. Companies must inform data subjects about how and why their information will be used, allowing them to choose about the collection and processing of their data.

2. Purpose and Data Minimization: The LGPD requires that personal data be collected and processed only for specific and legitimate purposes, and the amount of data collected must be limited to the minimum necessary to fulfill this purpose. This prevents the abusive use of personal data by companies.

3. Rights of Data Subjects: The LGPD also gives data subjects the right to access, correct, delete, and report their information, rights similar to those guaranteed by the GDPR. They may also object to the use of their data for certain purposes, such as direct marketing.

4. Flexibility for Public Security: One of the most notable differences between the LGPD and the GDPR is the flexibility granted by Brazilian law for the use of data in cases of public security, national defense, and crime investigation. These situations allow the processing of data without the need for explicit consent from the data subject, something that is not so broadly provided for in the GDPR.

5. Data Protection Officer (DPO): As with the GDPR, the LGPD requires large companies or companies that systematically process sensitive data to appoint a Data Protection Officer (DPO). The DPO is responsible for ensuring compliance with the law, as well as serving as a point of contact between the company, data subjects, and the National Data Protection Authority (ANPD).

6. Sanctions and Fines: The LGPD provides for administrative sanctions that can reach up to 2% of the company's annual revenue, limited to BRL 50 million per violation, similar to the model of financial sanctions imposed by the GDPR in the European Union. Although severe, these sanctions are intended to encourage compliance and increase the security of consumer data.

Impact on the Telecommunications Sector

Telecommunications operators, as they handle a huge volume of personal data, including sensitive data (such as location, consumer behavior, and financial information), were heavily impacted by the LGPD.

Companies such as Vivo, Oi, Claro, and TIM needed to make significant changes to their operations to ensure compliance with the new legislation. Some of the main impacts were:

1. Processing of Sensitive Data: The LGPD defines sensitive data as those related to racial origin, religious beliefs, health data, sexual orientation, among others.
Operators have had to review their policies and practices to ensure that this data is treated in accordance with the legislation, which includes the need for express consent and stricter treatment in terms of security.

2. Data Sharing between Third Parties: Before the LGPD, it was common for telecommunications operators to share their customers' data with business partners and marketing companies. The

LGPD imposed stricter restrictions on this type of sharing, requiring specific consent for the use of data by third parties.

3. Compliance Audits and Reports: To demonstrate compliance with the LGPD, operators started to conduct internal audits and establish compliance monitoring and reporting mechanisms. These audits include analyzing the life cycle of the data, from its collection to its disposal, and verifying that the rights of the subjects are being respected.

4. Employee Training: Companies in the telecommunications sector also needed to invest in training their teams on data protection best practices and the importance of following the principles of the LGPD. This education process is critical to ensuring that all levels of the organization are aligned with legal requirements.

Practical Example: Vivo and Oi

Brazilian operators Vivo and Oi were some of the most prominent in the effort to ensure compliance with the LGPD. Both have implemented a series of internal policies to strengthen the protection of personal data:

- Vivo: Vivo, the largest operator in Brazil, has invested heavily in digital security infrastructure and established a privacy center for its customers. The company has also created a direct channel for consumers to access and control their personal information, exercising their rights guaranteed by the LGPD, such as correcting data and deleting unnecessary information.

- Oi: Oi has also made major operational changes to ensure compliance with the LGPD. This included reviewing its contracts with third-party partners and implementing a policy of consent for the use of data, both for new customers and the existing customer base. In addition, Oi invested in privacy awareness campaigns for its consumers, highlighting the importance of personal data protection.

These efforts by Brazilian operators have not only ensured compliance with the LGPD, but have also improved consumers' trust in the way their data is handled, strengthening the relationship between companies and their customers in an increasingly regulated digital environment.

2.3 CCPA (California Consumer Privacy Act) – EUA

The California Consumer Privacy Act (CCPA), in effect since 2020, is one of the most comprehensive privacy laws in the United States, designed to protect California consumers and set new standards for how companies collect, store, and use personal data.

With a focus on large volumes of data, the CCPA offers additional rights to consumers, elevating the control individuals have over their personal information.

Basic Principles

The CCPA introduces several consumer protections and rights, which have a direct impact on companies in the telecommunications sector, including carriers that often handle large amounts of personal data, such as call history, location, and browsing preferences. The main rights established by the CCPA are:

1. Right to Know: Consumers have the right to know what data is being collected, how it is used, and with whom it is shared. Companies are required to provide this information upon request.

2. Right to Opt-Out: One of the strongest rights of the CCPA is the consumer's right to opt out of the sale of their personal data. Companies should offer a clear and easy way for consumers to exercise this option, such as through a visible "Do Not Sell My Data" button.

3. Right to Erasure (Erase Information): The consumer also has the right to request deletion of their personal data from the company's systems, unless such data is necessary to complete transactions or meet other legal obligations.

4. Right of Access: Consumers can request a copy of the personal data a company holds about them, as well as detailed information about how that data has been used or shared.

Impact on Telecom Operators

Major U.S. telecom carriers such as AT&T and Verizon have had to adjust their privacy policies and invest significantly in data security infrastructure to ensure CCPA compliance.

Since these companies handle massive volumes of data, the challenges to implementing CCPA requirements were significant, especially in the protection and monitoring of sensitive data.

- AT&T: AT&T, one of the largest telecommunications carriers in the U.S., has revised its data collection policies to provide additional transparency to consumers.

This has included creating online tools that allow users to view and control what data is being collected, as well as offering a simple way to opt out of sharing this information with third parties.

- Verizon: Verizon has implemented a number of technological and procedural changes to ensure CCPA compliance. The company has invested in encryption technology and access monitoring tools to better protect customer data.

In addition, as a way to meet the "no data sale" requirement, Verizon has developed easy options for consumers to manage their privacy preferences directly on their mobile devices.

Case Study: Compliance and Innovation

To ensure compliance, AT&T and Verizon have also adopted consent management systems, which track privacy choices made by consumers and automatically apply chosen preferences across the organization.

These operators needed to align CCPA compliance with technology innovation efforts, maintaining the balance between the use of data for service personalization and customer privacy.

2.4 Personal Data Protection Law in Angola (Law No. 22/11)

Angola's Law No. 22/11 on the Protection of Personal Data establishes the legal framework for the protection of personal data in the country, ensuring that the privacy rights of individuals are respected, especially in critical sectors such as telecommunications and energy.

The legislation follows international standards and requires companies to be more transparent and secure in handling data, especially sensitive data such as financial and biometric information.

Local Obligations and Challenges

The law imposes several obligations on companies operating in Angola, with a special focus on the collection, storage and processing of personal data. Key requirements include:

DATA PROTECTION AND SECURITY IN THE TELECOMMUNICATIONS SECTOR
CHALLENGES AND SOLUTIONS IN THE DIGITAL AGE

1. Clear Consent: Companies must obtain explicit consent from individuals to collect, process, and store their data. This consent should be free, informed, and specific, and individuals should have the option to revoke it at any time.

2. Data Security: The law requires companies to implement stringent security measures to protect data from unauthorized access, breaches, or misuse. This includes the use of encryption, access control, and regular audits.

3. Breach Notification: As with European legislation, companies in Angola are required to notify the National Data Protection Commission (CNPD) in the event of a data breach. This is to ensure that security breaches are dealt with effectively and that affected data subjects are informed quickly.

4. Rights of Data Subjects: Individuals have the right to access, rectify, and request deletion of their personal data. In addition, they have the right to be informed about how their data will be processed and for what purpose.

Case Studies

Telecommunications and energy companies, such as Sonangol and Unitel, have adjusted their operations to meet the requirements of Law No. 22/11 by implementing robust compliance practices and data protection mechanisms.

- Sonangol: Angola's largest oil and gas company, Sonangol, which processes data from thousands of employees and customers, had to conduct a thorough review of its data protection policies.

The company has invested in new encryption technologies and data security systems, as well as creating a department dedicated to data protection and compliance.

- Unitel: Angola's largest telecommunications operator, Unitel, has also taken steps to ensure compliance with the law.

The company has implemented internal processes to monitor the use of personal data and train its employees on the importance of following data protection regulations.

Unitel has invested in new security infrastructure, such as intrusion prevention systems and regular compliance audits.

Both the CCPA in the United States and the Personal Data Protection Act in Angola require companies to prioritize consumer privacy and take strict measures to ensure compliance.

These examples show that, despite regional differences, the global trend is clear: data protection has become an essential part of the operation of companies, especially in the telecommunications sector.

Adapting to these new rules is crucial not only to avoid sanctions, but to build trust with consumers in an increasingly connected digital world.

Chapter 3: Cybersecurity and Data Protection in the Telecommunications Sector

The telecommunications sector is one of the pillars of modern digital infrastructure, facilitating communication and data exchange on a global scale. However, this vitality also makes it an attractive target for cybercriminals.

In this chapter, we will examine the cyber risks that threaten the industry, the security measures that businesses can take to protect consumer data, and the importance of compliance with data protection regulations.

3.1 Cyber Risks and Threats in the Telecommunications Sector

Telecommunications are particularly vulnerable to a variety of cyberattacks. Among the most common risks are:

3.1.1 Phishing

Phishing is one of the most frequent methods of information theft. In this type of attack, cybercriminals send emails or messages that appear to be from trusted sources, such as banks, telecommunications operators, or online services, tricking users into providing personal information, such as passwords and bank details.

This method is effective because of its simplicity and the ease with which users can be fooled.

- Techniques Used: Attackers often use social engineering techniques, creating a false sense of urgency or need for action. For example, they may state that the user's account will be locked unless the user clicks on a link and provides their information.

- Impact: The impact of phishing can be devastating, leading to significant financial losses for consumers and data breaches for businesses, which can be held responsible for failing to protect their customers' information.

3.1.2 Ransomware

Ransomware is a type of cyberattack where cybercriminals block access to critical data by encrypting it until a ransom is paid. This method has become one of the biggest threats to companies in various sectors, especially telecommunications.

- Growth of Attacks: The frequency and sophistication of ransomware attacks have increased dramatically. In many cases, criminals not only demand payment in cryptocurrencies, but also threaten to leak the data if the ransom is not paid, which amplifies the risk for companies.

- Impact: The impact of a ransomware attack can be devastating, as businesses can lose valuable data and face significant disruptions to their operations. Additionally, recovery after an attack can be long and costly, requiring significant investments in technology and personnel.

3.1.3 DDoS (Distributed Denial of Service)

DDoS attacks involve overloading a network or service with an excessive volume of traffic, making it inaccessible to legitimate users.

These attacks are often used as a form of blackmail or to divert attention from other types of cyberattacks.

Telecommunications, which depend on the constant availability of services, are preferred targets for these attacks.

- Mechanism of Operation: DDoS attacks are carried out through botnets, which are networks of compromised devices.

Attackers send commands to these devices so that they all access a single target simultaneously, flooding it with requests and causing the service to fail.

- Consequences: The impact of a DDoS attack can be significant, resulting in lost revenue and reputational damage to the company.

Telecom operators facing service disruptions could lose customers and face regulatory fines.

3.1.4 Software and Hardware Vulnerabilities

Telecommunications also face risks arising from vulnerabilities in software and hardware. Outdated systems, misconfigured applications, and security flaws in network devices can be exploited by cybercriminals to access sensitive networks and data.

- Cybercriminals such as Vulnerability Exploiters: Attackers can utilize automated tools to scan networks for vulnerable devices.

Once they find a flaw, they can exploit that vulnerability to carry out attacks, such as installing malware or unauthorized access to sensitive data.

- Consequences: Exploiting vulnerabilities can result in significant financial losses, data breaches, and reputational damage.

The need for constant updates and security patches is critical for the protection of telecommunications infrastructures.

3.1.5 Insider Threats

Insider threats refer to risks originated by employees or former employees of the company who have access to sensitive systems and information.

These individuals may intentionally or accidentally compromise data security.

- Motivations for Insider Threats: Motivations can vary, including displeasure at work, attempts to steal data, or simple negligence regarding security practices.

- Consequences: The consequences of internal threats can be just as devastating as external ones, leading to data loss, information leaks, and damage to the company's reputation. Early detection and effective management of these risks are essential to mitigate the damage.

3.2 Security Measures to Protect Consumer Data

To address these cyber risks, telcos need to take a proactive approach to their security strategies. Key security measures include:

3.2.1 Encryption

Encryption is a key technique for protecting data, both in transit and at rest. By encrypting sensitive data, companies can ensure that even if this data is intercepted or accessed in an unauthorized manner, it remains unreadable to those who do not have the decryption key.

- Implementation of Encryption: Telecommunications must utilize robust encryption to protect data such as account information, call history, and user location.

3.2.2 Intrusion Monitoring and Detection

Implementing intrusion monitoring and detection systems (IDS/IPS) is crucial for identifying suspicious activity in real-time.

These systems can alert security teams to unauthorized access attempts, allowing for rapid response to incidents.

- Behavior Analysis: In addition to monitoring known activities, companies should implement behavior analysis to identify anomalous patterns that may indicate a breach.

3.2.3 Employee Training

Employees play a critical role in cybersecurity. Regular training on security practices and awareness of phishing and other social engineering tactics is critical to reducing the risk of successful attacks.

- Phishing simulations: Conducting phishing simulations can help train employees to recognize fraud attempts and improve staff response to security incidents.

3.2.4 Security Updates and Patches

Keeping all systems and software up to date is vital to protecting telecommunications from known vulnerabilities. Businesses should implement a regular schedule of updates and security patches.

- Vulnerability Management: Conducting security assessments and penetration testing can help identify and remediate vulnerabilities before they can be exploited by attackers.

3.2.5 Compliance with Data Protection Regulations

Telecommunications companies must ensure compliance with data protection regulations, such as LGPD in Brazil, CCPA in California, and Law No. 22/11 in Angola. Compliance not only protects consumers' data, but also prevents legal sanctions and reputational damage.

- Regular Audits: Conducting regular audits to ensure that security practices and data protection policies are aligned with regulations is essential to ensure ongoing compliance.

3.3 Importance of Compliance with Data Protection Regulations

Compliance with data protection regulations is not just a legal obligation, but a strategic necessity for telecommunications companies. The main reasons for the importance of compliance include:

3.3.1 Consumer Protection

Compliance with data protection regulations helps to ensure that consumers' rights are respected and that their personal information is handled responsibly. This promotes consumer trust in the company and its services.

3.3.2 Mitigation of Legal Risks

Failure to comply with regulations can result in severe penalties, including substantial fines and reputational damage. Companies that invest in compliance minimize these risks and avoid potential financial consequences.

3.3.3 Strengthening Brand Reputation

Companies that demonstrate a commitment to data protection and consumer privacy tend to have a stronger reputation. This can result in increased customer loyalty and competitive advantage in the market.

3.3.4 International Business Facilitation

Compliance with global data protection standards can make it easier to conduct business on an international scale, allowing companies to meet regulatory requirements in different jurisdictions.

3.4 Conclusion

Cybersecurity and data protection are essential to the integrity and continuity of the telecommunications industry. As cyber risks evolve, businesses must remain vigilant and proactive in their security approaches.

Implementing robust security measures, coupled with compliance with data protection regulations, not only protects consumers' data but also builds a strong foundation for brand trust and reputation.

In an ever-changing digital world, cybersecurity should be a top priority for all businesses operating in the telecommunications industry.

3.5 Security Measures for Data Protection

To mitigate the cyber risks mentioned earlier, telecommunications companies must adopt a series of robust security measures that aim to protect consumer data and ensure the integrity of their operations.

The increasing sophistication of attacks requires a multi-layered approach, combining advanced technologies with strict security policies. Below are the main measures that telecommunications companies implement to ensure data protection:

3.5.1 Encryption

Encryption is an essential technique for protecting data both in transit (when it's being transferred between devices) and at rest (when stored on systems or servers).

With encryption, even if data is intercepted or accessed by attackers, it remains unreadable without the proper keys to decrypt the information.

This protection is especially important in telecommunications environments, where large volumes of personal data, such as call history, geolocation, and account information, are transmitted on a regular basis.

- Data in Transit Encryption: Protects data as it is transferred between devices, networks, and servers. This includes the use of protocols such as TLS (Transport Layer Security), which ensures the confidentiality and integrity of communications.

- Data at Rest Encryption: Prevents stored data from being accessed by unauthorized users by using robust encryption algorithms to encode sensitive information.

3.5.2 Firewalls

Firewalls are one of the first lines of defense in telecommunications networks. They act as a barrier between the company's internal network and external networks, filtering data traffic based on a set of predefined rules.

This prevents unauthorized or malicious access from reaching the company's internal systems.

- Next-Generation Firewalls (NGFW): These integrate advanced packet inspection, intrusion detection, and additional security capabilities, enabling a more dynamic defense against complex cyberattacks.

- Web Application Firewalls (WAF): Protect web applications and services from specific threats, such as SQL injection attacks or malicious scripts, by filtering HTTP requests.

3.5.3 Zero-Trust Policies

Zero-Trust policies represent a significant shift in the way companies handle the security of their networks.

Instead of implicitly trusting any device or user within the network, as occurs in traditional approaches, the Zero-Trust model operates on the premise that no entity should be trusted by default, regardless of its location or previous credentials.

Each access request must be verified, authenticated, and authorized individually, ensuring that only legitimate users and devices can access sensitive data and systems.

- Continuous Verification: The Zero-Trust policy requires continuous verification of all devices and users, implementing multi-factor authentication (MFA) and real-time inspection of all network connections.

- Identity-Based Security: With each request, factors such as the user's identity, the device used, and geographic location are analyzed to ensure that access is granted based on the context and predefined security policies.

3.5.4 Network Segmentation

Network segmentation involves dividing IT infrastructure into different segments, or zones, that have different levels of access and protection.

This prevents an attacker who manages to compromise a part of the network from having unrestricted access to the entire infrastructure. Segmentation is crucial in telecommunications environments, where data circulation is constant and voluminous.

- Sensitive Data Isolation: Segmentation allows critical data, such as customer and infrastructure information, to be isolated from the rest of the network, making it difficult for attackers to access this information.

- Incident Containment: In the event of a security breach, segmentation helps limit the damage by restricting the attacker's access to only the compromised segment.

3.5.5 Continuous Monitoring and Threat Detection

Continuous monitoring of systems and networks is critical to identifying suspicious activity and responding quickly to security incidents.

Telecommunications companies need advanced intrusion detection (IDS) and intrusion prevention (IPS) systems to monitor traffic in real time and identify anomalous behavior that may indicate attack attempts.

- Behavioral Analysis: In addition to monitoring known activities, companies should utilize artificial intelligence and machine learning to identify anomalous patterns of behavior, such as unusual access or unauthorized data transfers.

- Incident Response: Automated incident response systems can help mitigate attacks quickly by blocking malicious access and implementing countermeasures before the damage spreads.

3.5.6 Security Updates and Patches

Keeping systems and software up-to-date is one of the most important measures to protect telecommunications networks from known vulnerabilities.

Flaw exploits in outdated software are one of the main gateways for cybercriminals.

- Vulnerability Management: Companies should conduct periodic audits and penetration tests to identify and fix vulnerabilities before they are exploited.

- Patching Policies: Implement a strict security patching schedule on all critical systems to ensure they are protected from the latest threats.

3.5.7 Employee Training

Employee awareness and training is crucial for preventing cyberattacks. Employees are often the weakest link in a company's security, being susceptible to social engineering attacks such as phishing.

Investing in regular training can significantly reduce the risks of security breaches.

- Phishing simulations: Companies can conduct phishing attack simulations to train their employees to recognize and avoid threats.

- Good Security Practices: Employees should be regularly trained on security practices, such as using strong passwords, securing devices, and how to report suspicious activity.

3.5.8 Data Backup and Recovery

Having a robust data backup and recovery plan is essential for mitigating the impacts of cyberattacks, such as ransomware.

Regular backups ensure that in the event of a successful attack, businesses can restore their operations quickly without paying ransoms.

- Secure Backup Storage: Maintain copies of encrypted backups in separate locations from the main network, ensuring that in the event of a compromise, data can be safely restored.

- Regular Recovery Testing: Regularly test recovery procedures to ensure that backups are functional and can be restored quickly after an incident.

3.5.9 Case Study: The Attack on TalkTalk

The cyberattack on TalkTalk, a UK telecoms operator, in 2015 highlighted the importance of maintaining robust and up-to-date security systems.

In this incident, cybercriminals exploited a vulnerability in an outdated system, which resulted in the leakage of personal data of more than 157,000 customers, including banking information.

The security flaw exposed the lack of proper encryption to protect this critical data, which facilitated the success of the attack.

- Consequences of the Attack: As a result, TalkTalk faced a fine of £400,000 imposed by the Information Commissioner's Office (ICO), as well as suffering significant losses to its reputation.

The company was forced to completely overhaul its security policies, implementing new measures such as hardened encryption, continuous monitoring systems, and security awareness trainings for its employees.

This case underlines the importance of continuous and adaptive security measures, especially in an industry as critical as telecommunications.

Staying one step ahead of cyber threats is essential for protecting consumer data and the integrity of business operations.

3.6 Compliance with Data Protection Regulations

Compliance with data protection regulations is crucial for telecommunications companies, not only to avoid penalties but also to maintain consumer confidence.

To ensure that they are compliant with regulations such as GDPR, LGPD, and CCPA, many companies implement strict compliance practices.

Companies like Vodafone conduct regular audits and training for their employees. These audits assess the effectiveness of security policies and compliance with regulations.

Ongoing training is critical to ensure that all employees understand the importance of data security and their responsibilities in relation to it.

In addition, Vodafone has promoted transparency in its data processing practices, allowing consumers to know exactly how their information is being used.

This chapter emphasizes the critical intersection between cybersecurity and data protection in the telecommunications sector.

As the threat environment evolves, companies need to adapt and strengthen their defenses to protect not only their systems, but also the privacy and trust of their customers.

Implementing effective security measures and complying with data protection regulations are essential steps in addressing contemporary cyber challenges.

Chapter 4: Emerging Technologies: 5G, IoT, and the New Frontier of Privacy

The advancement of emerging technologies such as 5G networks and the Internet of Things (IoT) is reshaping the telecommunications landscape.

These technologies not only promote innovation but also raise significant issues related to data privacy and security.

In this chapter, we will examine how these new technologies are transforming the industry and what challenges they present.

4.1 5G Networks and the Impact on Data Collection

5G networks promise to revolutionize the way we connect, offering download speeds up to 100 times faster than 4G networks and allowing an exponential number of devices to connect simultaneously.

This enables advanced applications such as autonomous vehicles, smart cities, and digital health solutions.

However, this large-scale connectivity brings with it new vulnerabilities and challenges. The increase in the amount of data generated and transmitted by connected devices increases attack surfaces for cybercriminals. Some of the main concerns include:

- Increased Data Exposure: With more connected devices, users' personal data is at greater risk. Each additional device that connects to the network represents a new opportunity for hackers to exploit vulnerabilities.

- Device Interconnectivity: 5G will facilitate communication between devices in real-time, but this interconnectivity can create additional risks. A compromised device can serve as an entry point for attacks on other devices on the same network.

- Privacy and Consent: The massive collection of data generated by 5G devices raises questions about consent and privacy.

Companies must be transparent about how data is being collected, used, and shared, ensuring that users have control over their personal information.

In short, while 5G networks present significant opportunities for innovation, it is essential for telecommunications companies to implement robust security and data protection policies to mitigate the associated risks.

4.2 Internet of Things (IoT) and Telecommunications

The Internet of Things (IoT) is expanding rapidly, with the introduction of connected devices ranging from wearables such as smart watches to smart home appliances and medical devices.

These devices have the potential to significantly improve quality of life and operational efficiency. However, the growing adoption of IoT also brings serious concerns about data security and privacy.

4.2.1 IoT Challenges:

- Security Vulnerabilities: Many IoT devices are designed for convenience and functionality, but they often lack robust security measures. This can result in weaknesses that are exploited by attackers, putting users' data at risk.

- Sensitive Data Collection: Connected devices, especially in healthcare settings, can collect a significant amount of personal and sensitive data. Without proper protection, this data can be accessed or misused.

- Lack of Standardization: The diversity of devices and manufacturers in the IoT ecosystem makes it difficult to implement consistent security standards.

Each manufacturer may have different approaches to security and privacy, making the landscape even more complex.

Case Study: Data Leaks in Medical Devices

A worrying example of IoT's impact on privacy is the data leakage associated with connected medical devices.

In several cases, devices such as glucose monitors and pacemakers, which transmit real-time health information to healthcare providers, were found to have security flaws that allowed unauthorized access.

One specific study revealed that sensitive patient information was being exposed through telecommunications networks due to vulnerabilities in the communication protocols used by the devices.

Not only do these incidents put patients' privacy at risk, but they also raise questions about the responsibility of telecommunications companies and device manufacturers to ensure data security.

5. Chapter Summary

In this chapter, we discuss how emerging technologies such as 5G and IoT are transforming the telecommunications industry and what the challenges are related to data privacy and security.

The speed and connectivity provided by 5G, along with the increased use of IoT devices, present a new frontier in terms of data collection and its implications.

Telecommunications companies must be prepared to address these issues and implement effective policies that protect user data, ensuring a secure transition to this new digital era.

Chapter 5: Advantages and Disadvantages of Strict Data Protection

Data protection is one of the fundamental pillars of the operation of telecommunications companies in the digital age, being both a legal requirement and a growing expectation of consumers.

While data protection legislations such as GDPR in Europe, LGPD in Brazil, and CCPA in California have set a global compliance standard, companies face a number of advantages and disadvantages when implementing strict data protection policies.

This chapter explores in detail the benefits and challenges associated with these practices, providing a comprehensive overview of the impact of these measures on both organizations and consumers.

5.1 Advantages

The implementation of strict data protection measures brings a series of strategic, operational, and reputational benefits to telecommunications companies, in addition to promoting greater security for consumers.

5.1.1 Consumer Confidence

Building trust with consumers is one of the main advantages of implementing a robust data protection policy.

In an increasingly digitized environment, where personal data is at risk due to breaches, cyberattacks, and misuse by businesses, consumers have become more discerning about the way their information is handled.

- Loyalty and Increased Sales: Companies that demonstrate a commitment to data privacy and security tend to gain customer loyalty.

When consumers feel that their information is protected and that their privacy rights are being respected, they are more willing to share data and interact with the company.

This trust translates into higher customer retention and potentially an increase in sales, as confident consumers are more likely to purchase new services or products.

- Brand Reputation: Efficient data protection contributes directly to a brand's reputation. Companies that prioritize privacy and security are viewed more positively in the market, especially in competitive industries such as telecommunications.

Research shows that 90% of consumers prefer to do business with companies that have a good reputation regarding data protection, which can become a significant competitive advantage.

5.1.2 Prevention of Fines and Sanctions

Compliance with data protection regulations is crucial to avoid severe financial penalties.

Laws such as GDPR, LGPD, and CCPA impose fines that can reach exorbitant amounts in cases of non-compliance, data leaks, or failures to provide privacy rights to consumers.

- Avoid Financial Penalties: Fines can be devastating for businesses, both financially and reputationally.

One notorious example is British Airways, which faced a £183 million fine for a data breach that exposed sensitive information of hundreds of thousands of customers.

Avoiding this type of sanction through a robust data protection system is therefore a priority for companies operating globally.

- Business Stability and Sustainability: Compliance with data protection laws ensures not only the company's legal certainty, but also its long-term sustainability.

By mitigating the risk of litigation and sanctions, businesses can focus on developing their operations, expanding their services, and maintaining market confidence.

5.1.3 Improvement of Internal Processes

Adopting strict data protection policies can generate significant improvements in an organization's internal processes, encouraging an organizational culture focused on accountability, transparency, and efficiency.

- Increased Operational Efficiency: Implementing more robust data management practices results in a more disciplined and efficient organizational structure.

Processes such as the Data Protection Impact Assessment (DPIA), required by the GDPR for activities involving sensitive data, encourage companies to evaluate and optimize the way they collect, store, and use information.

- Positive Organizational Culture: Data protection promotes a culture of ethics and responsibility. Employees who are trained in information security best practices are more aware of the importance of protecting customer data, which raises the ethical standard of the organization as a whole.

This type of environment can also attract skilled talent, who identify with companies that adhere to high compliance and privacy standards.

5.1.4 Competitive Advantage in Digital Markets

In a digital transformation landscape, where data collection and analysis play a central role, effective protection of sensitive information can become a significant competitive advantage.

Companies that stand out for their compliance with data privacy and security are often preferred by consumers and business partners.

- Attractiveness to Partners: Organizations that maintain high-level data protection policies may also attract partnerships with other companies or investors who value privacy compliance as a key criterion.

This is especially true in international markets, where compliance requirements are stringent.

5.2 Disadvantages

Despite the substantial benefits, implementing stringent data protection policies also presents challenges and drawbacks, especially for businesses that operate in multiple jurisdictions or face resource limitations.

5.2.1 Cost of Implementation

One of the main challenges associated with strict data protection is the significant cost of implementation. For many companies, especially small and medium-sized ones, adapting to complex regulations can require considerable financial investments.

- Investment in IT Infrastructure: The need to upgrade and maintain IT systems that are compliant with data protection regulations can be burdensome.

This includes implementing security technologies such as encryption, advanced firewalls, and real-time data monitoring solutions.

- Training and Enablement: Ongoing training of employees at all levels is essential to ensure that everyone understands the company's obligations in terms of data protection.

These training programs, while necessary, pose additional costs that can be challenging for smaller companies, which often lack a robust compliance framework.

5.2.2 Regulatory Complexity

The multitude of global data protection regulations creates a complex legal and operational landscape for companies operating in multiple markets.

Each region may have its own privacy laws and guidelines, such as GDPR in Europe, LGPD in Brazil, and CCPA in California, with specific requirements that need to be strictly followed.

- Legal Confusion: Complying with different regulations can result in confusion about which practices should be adopted, especially when laws are contradictory or require different approaches to data protection.

This increases the need for constant legal advice and an in-house team that specializes in privacy.

- Operational Difficulties: Maintaining compliance with different regulations requires continuous monitoring and flexible data governance processes that can be adapted to changing laws in each jurisdiction.

This constant effort to adapt can consume significant resources and hinder operational efficiency.

5.2.3 Impact on Innovation

Strict data protection, while necessary for security and privacy, can in some cases restrict innovation, particularly in industries that rely on data analytics to develop new products and services.

- Limitations on Product Development: The requirement for explicit consent for data collection and the right of consumers to delete their information can limit the amount of data available to businesses.

In areas such as big data, artificial intelligence, and predictive analytics, where large volumes of data are needed to generate valuable insights, this limitation can slow down the development of new data-driven solutions or products.

- Reduced Exploitation of New Technologies: The fear of violating privacy laws can discourage companies from exploring new technologies, such as blockchain or IoT, that rely on collecting and processing large amounts of information.

Companies can opt for safer but less innovative solutions to avoid potential regulatory complications, thereby limiting innovation.

5.2.4 Bureaucratization and Slowness in Processes

Increasing data protection regulations can lead to excessive bureaucratization within companies, with slower and more complex processes for handling data processing.

- Delays in Business Processes: Companies need to constantly review their data collection and handling practices, which can slow down the launch of new services or products in the market.

The need to perform DPIAs or obtain multiple authorizations for data processing can prolong development time, impacting business agility.

- Need for Continuous Oversight: Compliance requires constant oversight by dedicated teams, such as Data Protection Officers (DPOs), which can overwhelm management and increase operational costs.

5.3 Chapter Summary

In this chapter, we discuss the advantages and disadvantages of implementing strict data protection policies.

While robust data protection offers clear benefits, such as strengthening consumer trust, preventing fines, and improving internal processes, it also comes with substantial challenges, including high implementation costs, regulatory complexity, impact on innovation, and bureaucratization of processes.

For telcos, the challenge is to strike a balance between the need to protect data and opportunities for innovation, maximising the benefits of compliance while mitigating financial and operational challenges.

Chapter 6: Integration between Data Regulation and Telecommunications Expansion Policy

The advancement of telecommunications, driven by technologies such as 5G and the Internet of Things (IoT), marks an era of global transformations, offering new opportunities for connectivity and innovation.

However, this progress also brings significant challenges related to the protection of consumer data.

This chapter explores the intersection between telecommunications expansion and data protection regulations, highlighting the importance of public-private partnerships to address these challenges effectively and responsibly.

6.1 The Relationship between the Growth of Telecommunications and Data Protection

The introduction of 5G networks and interconnected devices through IoT is rapidly expanding telecom capacity while increasing the collection and processing of personal data on a large scale.

The development of more robust and connected infrastructures presents a critical intersection between technological innovation and data protection requirements.

For this evolution to occur in a secure manner and in compliance with privacy regulations, it is necessary to balance technological advancement with solid data governance.

6.1.1 Compliance Challenges in Expanding Networks

Technological expansion requires telecommunications companies to adapt to new regulatory compliance challenges.

- Increased Collection of Personal Data: 5G and IoT enable the connection of a vast array of devices – from smartphones to self-driving cars to smart home appliances – resulting in unprecedented data collection.

This includes sensitive personal information, such as biometric data, spending habits, and geographic location. Ensuring that the processing of this data meets global regulations such as GDPR, LGPD, and CCPA becomes a central priority for operators.

- Extended Liability: Carriers not only facilitate the transmission of data, but take responsibility for protecting that information.

More complex networks, such as 5G, with millions of connected devices, increase vulnerability to security breaches, making it critical to adopt rigorous protection practices.

- Multi-jurisdictional regulations: For operators operating in different regions, compliance with various national and local regulations is an ongoing challenge.

The complexity of these requirements increases the need for a coordinated approach that harmonises data protection practices globally.

6.1.2 Responsible Innovation and Data Protection

Technological innovation must go hand in hand with ethical responsibility and data protection.

- Privacy by Design: The privacy-by-design approach is critical to ensuring that data protection is embedded in all phases of new service and product development.

By adopting this principle, operators ensure that 5G networks and IoT devices are aligned with security best practices.

- National Security and Critical Infrastructure: In addition to individual privacy, the expansion of telecommunications raises concerns about national security, as complex networks become targets for cyberattacks, potentially compromising critical sectors such as energy and transportation.

- Ethical Use of Data: The collection of personal data for business purposes must be done ethically and transparently. Practices such as ad personalization and the use of behavioral data need to be based on clear consent from users.

6.1.3 Benefits of Compliance in Technological Expansion

Compliance with data protection regulations should not only be seen as a legal obligation, but also as an opportunity to gain competitive advantages and strengthen consumer confidence.

- Competitive Advantage: Companies that demonstrate commitment to data protection gain the trust of consumers and partners, differentiating themselves positively in the market.

- Secure Innovations: Compliance with regulations spurs the development of secure innovations, such as telemedicine, smart cities, and autonomous vehicles, where data security is a key requirement.

6.2 The Importance of Public-Private Partnerships

To achieve an effective balance between innovation and data protection in the expansion of telecommunications, collaboration between the public and private sectors is essential.

These partnerships foster a regulatory environment conducive to responsible innovation, while ensuring the safety and privacy of consumers.

6.2.1 Effective Policy Development

The creation of sound data protection policies is fundamental for the advancement of telecommunications.

- Open and Collaborative Dialogue: Ongoing dialogue between telecommunications companies and governments allows for the formulation of proactive regulations that protect data privacy without stifling innovation.

- Regulatory Flexibility: Flexible policies ensure that operators can innovate while maintaining compliance with regulations, balancing technological growth and social responsibility.

6.2.2 Education and Awareness

Educating consumers about privacy and data protection is a pillar for building a secure ecosystem.

- Joint Awareness Campaigns: Governments and companies can collaborate on awareness campaigns, informing consumers about their rights and how to protect their personal data.

- Privacy Control Tools: Offering tools that allow users to manage their data sharing preferences strengthens transparency and consumers' control over their information.

6.2.3 Development of Secure Technologies

The creation of secure networks depends on the integration of privacy principles from the beginning of the development of new technologies.

- Privacy by Design: Adopting privacy-by-design principles in emerging technologies ensures that data protection is a priority from planning to implementation.

- Investment in Research and Development (R&D): Public-private partnerships can foster investments in R&D, resulting in technological innovations that reconcile performance and security, such as advanced encryption systems and anonymization tools.

6.2.4 Rapid Incident Responses

In an increasingly interconnected landscape, rapid response to security incidents is essential.

- Joint Response Protocols: Coordinated protocols between the public and private sectors ensure quick and efficient action in the event of cyberattacks, minimizing damage and protecting consumers.

- Intelligence Exchange: The sharing of information on cyber threats between companies and governments strengthens the prevention and response to incidents, promoting more robust collective security.

6.3 Chapter Summary

This chapter addressed the relationship between telecommunications expansion and data protection, highlighting the importance of public-private partnerships to ensure secure and regulatory-compliant growth.

Collaboration between governments and businesses is essential for developing effective policies, raising consumer awareness, and creating safe technologies.

By integrating privacy and innovation, these partnerships ensure that the future of telecommunications is guided by ethical principles, trust, and security.

Chapter 7: Conclusions and Recommendations

This final chapter aims to reflect on the main points discussed throughout the book and present practical recommendations for the future of data protection in the telecommunications sector.

The increasing complexity of the digital environment, driven by emerging technologies such as Artificial Intelligence (AI), 5G networks, and the Internet of Things (IoT), poses unprecedented challenges and opportunities.

Ensuring effective data protection is a central issue in this scenario, which requires continuous adaptation by companies, governments and consumers.

7.1 The Future of Data Protection in the Telecommunications Industry

DATA PROTECTION AND SECURITY IN THE TELECOMMUNICATIONS SECTOR
CHALLENGES AND SOLUTIONS IN THE DIGITAL AGE

Technological evolution is transforming telecommunications into an essential sector for the digital economy.

However, this transformation comes with substantial risks to the privacy and security of personal data.

The future of data protection in the telecommunications sector will be shaped by the ability of all actors involved – from regulators to consumers – to collaborate to address these challenges.

Ongoing Dialogue

Continuous dialogue between telecommunications companies, regulatory bodies, and consumers is crucial to ensure that data protection is effective and accompanied by technological innovation.

The speed at which new technologies, such as AI and 5G, are being implemented demands that regulations be continuously reviewed and updated.

- Engagement with Consumers: Consumer expectations regarding privacy are changing. With the growing awareness of the risks associated with data collection, consumers are becoming more demanding about security practices.

Companies need to maintain constant engagement with their customers, clarifying how their data is collected, stored, and protected.

This transparency is essential for building trust and ensuring that consumers feel safe when sharing information.

- International Collaboration: As telecommunications are globalized, it is critical that dialogue includes international collaboration between regulators and companies from different countries.

Data protection laws, such as the GDPR in Europe and the LGPD in Brazil, have already demonstrated the need for a harmonized approach to addressing global privacy challenges.

Partnerships between countries and international organizations are essential to create consistent regulatory standards that are applicable to a globalized digital environment.

Adaptation of Regulations

As technology evolves, data protection regulations also need to adapt. Data collection through IoT-connected devices, AI-powered predictive analytics, and 5G interconnectivity bring new risks that require an overhaul of existing privacy policies.

- New Regulatory Models: Regulators must be willing to explore new regulatory models that allow for the flexibility needed to address emerging technologies.

This can include creating specific guidelines for AI and real-time data collection, requiring companies to implement robust data protection policies from the start of new service development.

In addition, the concept of agile regulation, which allows for rapid adjustments in response to technological innovations, should be widely considered.

- Data Protection in 5G and IoT Infrastructures: With the expansion of 5G infrastructure and the exponential increase in connected IoT devices, it is essential that regulations cover critical telecommunications infrastructures.

5G networks enable massive real-time data collection, which requires security policies to be adequate to prevent this data from being exploited by cybercriminals.

Security by design and privacy by default should be mandatory pillars in the construction of these new infrastructures.

Education and Awareness

One of the central challenges of data protection is consumers' lack of understanding of how their information is being handled.

Telecommunications companies, along with governments, should prioritize educating and raising public awareness of their privacy rights and the use of their data.

- Awareness Campaigns: In order for consumers to be able to make informed choices about their personal information, it is crucial that public education campaigns are launched, clarifying how companies use and protect this data.

Governments and private organizations can collaborate to create accessible educational content, clearly explaining the risks and rights of consumers in relation to privacy.

These campaigns should be conducted in a proactive manner, using digital communication channels and local events to reach different age groups and levels of technological familiarity.

- Privacy Control Tools: In addition to education, telecommunications companies should provide accessible and easy-to-use tools for consumers to manage their privacy preferences.

These tools should allow users to see exactly what data is being collected, how it's being used, and with whom it's being shared, offering a simple way to revoke or adjust those permissions.

7.2 Practical Recommendations for Telecommunications Companies

Based on the discussions throughout this book, we present some practical recommendations for telecommunications companies that want to adapt effectively to data protection regulations and new technologies.

1. Adopt Data Protection by Design: Companies should implement data protection from the earliest stages of developing new products and services.

This includes ensuring that all aspects of systems are designed with privacy in mind, minimizing data collection, and implementing robust encryption to protect sensitive information.

2. Invest in Cybersecurity: With the rise in cyber threats, it is imperative for telecommunications companies to make significant investments in cybersecurity.

This includes implementing real-time threat detection tools, empowering internal teams, and creating incident response protocols that are agile and efficient.

3. Ensure Multi-Jurisdictional Compliance: Companies operating in different countries must ensure that they are compliant with the various data protection laws in force, such as GDPR, LGPD, and CCPA.

This requires constant monitoring of regulatory changes and the development of compliance strategies that can be quickly adapted to new legislative environments.

4. Empower Employees in Data Protection: Ongoing training of employees on data protection principles and security best practices is essential to ensure that all members of the organization understand their responsibility in protecting personal information.

5. Promote Transparency with Consumers: Telecommunications companies should commit to full transparency regarding their use of data, clearly informing consumers about how their information is being handled, stored, and protected.

This not only increases customer confidence but also reduces the risk of legal action and regulatory sanctions.

Chapter Summary

In this last chapter, we discuss the future of data protection in the telecommunications sector, highlighting the importance of continuous dialogue between governments, companies and consumers, and the need to adapt regulations to new technologies.

Educating consumers and promoting transparency in privacy practices are also key aspects for the success of any data protection policy.

The practical recommendations presented here aim to help telecommunications companies prepare for future challenges by promoting a safer and more reliable digital environment for all involved.

The balance between innovation and data protection will be the foundation of a sustainable and ethical telecommunications sector in the digital age.

7.2 Practical Recommendations for Telecommunications Companies

Complying with data protection regulations and ensuring consumer privacy are growing challenges in the telecommunications industry, especially in the face of rapid technological evolution and increased data collection.

To address these challenges, companies need to adopt robust strategies that balance innovation and regulatory compliance, while ensuring security and transparency. The following are detailed practical recommendations to guide companies through this process.

Steps to Implement Compliance Policies

Implementing effective compliance policies is a multifaceted task that involves adopting appropriate practices, processes, and technologies to ensure that data is collected, stored, and used securely.

These steps are essential for aligning with regulations such as GDPR, LGPD, and CCPA, in addition to promoting good corporate governance practices.

1. Risk Assessment

The first step in ensuring compliance is to conduct a comprehensive risk assessment. This process should identify and map all areas where data collection, storage, and use are done in the organization. The risk assessment shall examine:

- Technological vulnerabilities that can be exploited by hackers or caused by human error.

- Data collection practices that may be in disagreement with regulations.

- Cross-border data transfer, which may require special attention to the data protection laws of different jurisdictions.

This assessment should be conducted regularly, especially as new technologies or processes are implemented.

2. Appointment of a Data Protection Officer (DPO)

Telecommunications companies, especially those that handle large volumes of personal data, must appoint a Data Protection Officer (DPO). The DPO is responsible for:

- Monitor compliance with data protection regulations.

- Develop and supervise data protection policies, including the response to breaches.

- Ensure clear communication with regulators, consumers, and stakeholders on privacy-related issues.

Additionally, the DPO serves as a central point of contact for consumers who want to exercise their rights, such as accessing data or requesting the removal of information.

3. Development of Clear Privacy Policies

Creating and maintaining transparent and accessible privacy policies is a legal obligation, but also an essential practice for building trust with consumers. Policies should:

- Explain how and why the data is collected.

- Describe how data is stored, shared, and secured.

- Provide information about consumers' rights and how they can access, correct, or delete their data.

These policies should be reviewed and updated regularly, especially when new technologies such as AI and IoT are integrated into operations.

4. Regular Audits and Monitoring

To ensure that data protection policies and practices are effectively implemented, companies should conduct regular internal and external audits. Audits should:

- Evaluate the performance of data protection systems.

- Identify areas where improvement is needed.

- Ensure that the company is in ongoing compliance with regulations and best practices.

These audits not only help maintain compliance but also promote an organizational culture of safety and accountability.

Best Practices to Ensure Data Security and Privacy

Protecting consumer data requires a comprehensive approach that goes beyond regulatory compliance. The best practices outlined below can help telcos mitigate risk, maintain consumer confidence, and create a resilient data infrastructure.

1. Ongoing Employee Training

Data security is only as strong as the weakest link. Therefore, it is crucial that all employees, from technical staff to customer service, receive ongoing training on:

- Data protection practices, such as the secure handling of personal information and the importance of minimizing access to sensitive data.

- Recognition of cyber threats, such as phishing, malware, and other tactics used by hackers.

- Incident response protocols, ensuring that in the event of a breach, staff are prepared to react quickly and effectively.

Training programs must also be adapted as new threats and regulations emerge.

2. Implementation of Advanced Security Technologies

Telecommunications companies must invest in advanced security technologies that protect consumer data from cyberattacks and other risks. This includes:

- Encryption: Utilize strong encryption for both data in transit and data at rest, ensuring that even in the event of improper access, the information is unusable.

- Multi-factor authentication (MFA): Strengthen the security of access to systems with multiple layers of authentication.

- Firewalls and intrusion prevention systems: Monitor and protect networks from unauthorized access.

- Continuous monitoring solutions: Implement tools that detect and respond to potential threats in real-time.

3. Transparency and Communication with Consumers

Maintaining transparency is essential to strengthen consumer trust. Companies must:

- Proactively inform consumers about their data collection and use practices.

- Facilitate access to information about how their data is used by providing clear options for consumers to manage their privacy preferences.

- Clearly communicate any incident or data breach, explaining the steps being taken to address the issue and protect consumers in the future.

4. Incident Response Plans

Even with the best security practices, data breaches can occur. Therefore, telecommunications companies need to have a robust incident response plan that includes:

- Rapid notification to consumers and regulators in the event of a data breach, meeting the required legal deadlines.

- Immediate containment and mitigation actions to minimize the impact of the breach.

- Post-incident analysis to identify the cause of the breach and take action to prevent it from occurring again.

A well-structured plan can significantly reduce the reputational and financial damage of a data breach.

Chapter Summary

This chapter concludes the discussion on data protection in the telecommunications sector by highlighting the importance of continuous dialogue between stakeholders and the need for constant adaptation to new technologies. The practical recommendations presented here provide a clear guide for companies to:

- Implement robust compliance policies.

- Ensure the security and privacy of consumer data.

- Educate and train their teams on data protection.

- Respond quickly to incidents, minimizing negative impacts.

By taking a proactive stance towards data protection, telecommunications companies can not only meet their legal obligations but also strengthen consumer trust, creating a sustainable competitive advantage in the market.

With a strong commitment to privacy, businesses can ensure their long-term success in an increasingly complex and challenging digital environment.

Chapter 8: Case Studies and Examples

In this chapter, we will explore a series of practical cases that illustrate the implementation of data protection legislation in different global contexts and the impacts of these laws on the operations of telecommunications companies.

Analyzing these cases provides a deeper understanding of the challenges faced by businesses, as well as the best practices adopted to ensure compliance and security of consumer data.

Case 1: GDPR Implementation in European Union Companies

The implementation of the General Data Protection Regulation (GDPR) in the European Union has caused a real revolution in the operations of telecommunications companies.

Context

The GDPR came into force in May 2018, establishing a set of strict guidelines for the collection and processing of personal data.

DATA PROTECTION AND SECURITY IN THE TELECOMMUNICATIONS SECTOR
CHALLENGES AND SOLUTIONS IN THE DIGITAL AGE

This regulation not only increased the responsibility of companies regarding the use of data, but also gave EU citizens greater control over their personal information.

Telecom operators, who handle large volumes of personal data, have had to reevaluate and restructure their practices to meet the new requirements.

Challenges

Operators have faced several significant challenges in implementing the GDPR, including:

- Collection of Explicit Consent: One of the strictest requirements of the GDPR is for companies to obtain explicit consent from customers before processing their personal data.

This required a shift in the approach to data collection, focusing on methods that ensured clarity and transparency for users.

- Data Protection Impact Assessments (DPIAs): Companies were required to conduct detailed assessments of how their data processes could impact users' privacy, especially in relation to sensitive data.

- Resources and Training: Many operators found that they needed substantial investments in training and resources to ensure that all employees were aware of the new guidelines and the importance of data protection.

Solution

Telecommunications company Telefónica exemplifies a successful approach to GDPR implementation:

1. Appointing DPOs: Telefónica has appointed Data Protection Officers (DPOs) to oversee GDPR compliance, offering a dedicated point of contact for privacy-related issues.

2. Employee Training: The operator developed a comprehensive training program, which included workshops and seminars to educate employees on the importance of data protection and how they could contribute to compliance.

3. Creation of Access Platforms: Telefónica implemented digital platforms that allowed users to access and manage their data easily and transparently, reinforcing customer confidence in the company's practices.

Results

Telefónica's actions resulted in significant positive results:

- Increased Consumer Trust: Research showed that more than 80% of customers felt secure about the company's protection of their data, a considerable increase compared to previous trust levels.

- Improved Reputation: Telefónica has become a benchmark in data protection in the sector, which has resulted in a substantial improvement in its public image and competitiveness in the market.

Case 2: Adjustments to the LGPD in Brazil

The General Data Protection Law (LGPD) came into force in Brazil in September 2020, imposing new obligations on telecommunications companies that handle personal data of Brazilian users.

Context

Brazilian operators, such as Oi and Vivo, had to adjust their data collection and processing practices to meet the requirements of the LGPD, which establishes principles such as the need for explicit consent and transparency in the use of data.

Challenges

Operators faced notable challenges, such as:

- Obtaining Consent: Obtaining explicit consent from users for the use of sensitive data, such as location and browsing history, has become a critical task, requiring more transparent and informative methods.

- Changes in Organizational Culture: Companies needed to promote an internal cultural change, where all employees were made aware of the importance of data protection.

- Systems Adaptation: Adapting existing IT systems to allow the management and secure storage of personal data required significant investments.

Solution

To comply with the LGPD, operators such as Oi and Vivo have implemented a series of solutions:

1. Consent Management Systems: Operators have implemented systems that have allowed users to manage their privacy preferences in a clear and accessible manner, ensuring that customers can easily give or withdraw their consent.

2. Regular Training: Oi and Vivo conducted regular training for their teams on the new regulations and best practices in data security, reinforcing the importance of compliance at all levels of the organization.

3. Awareness Campaigns: Operators launched awareness campaigns to educate consumers about their rights and how their data was being used.

Results

These adaptations have resulted in tangible benefits:

- Decrease in Complaints: There was a significant reduction in privacy-related complaints, with users reporting greater satisfaction with the handling of their data.

- Increased Customer Satisfaction: Surveys have indicated an increase in customer satisfaction, reflecting the effectiveness of the measures implemented and the positive perception of operators regarding data protection.

Case 3: CCPA's Impact on U.S. Carriers

The California Consumer Privacy Act (CCPA), which came into effect in January 2020, brought significant changes to telecom operators in the United States, altering the way consumer data is managed.

Context

The CCPA has imposed specific rights on California consumers regarding their personal data, emphasizing transparency and consumer control over the collection and use of their information.

Challenges

Carriers such as AT&T and Verizon faced the following challenges:

- Transparency in Policies: It was crucial to ensure that consumers could easily access information about what data was being collected and how it would be used, which required a comprehensive review of privacy policies.

- Integration of New Systems: Businesses needed to integrate new systems that would allow users to manage their privacy preferences, ensuring that these changes were implemented efficiently and effectively.

Solution

Operators have developed several innovative solutions:

1. Privacy Portals: AT&T and Verizon have created privacy portals that allow users to access their personal information, make data deletion requests, and manage privacy preferences in a clear and accessible manner.

2. Consumer Education Campaigns: Businesses have implemented education campaigns to raise awareness of consumer rights under the CCPA, utilizing a variety of channels such as email, social media, and direct ads.

3. Feedback and Reviews: Operators have established feedback channels that have allowed consumers to voice their concerns and suggestions, helping to continuously improve data protection practices.

Results

The implementation of the CCPA resulted in:

- Improved Consumer Trust: A study indicated that 75% of users felt more comfortable sharing their data with companies that respect their privacy options, reflecting an increase in consumer trust.

- Industry Recognition: AT&T and Verizon were recognized as leaders in privacy compliance, which not only enhanced their reputations but also brought new business opportunities.

Example 4: Sonangol and Unitel's compliance with Angola's Data Protection Law

The Personal Data Protection Law in Angola (Law No. 22/11) has presented significant challenges and opportunities for major telecom operators in the country, such as Sonangol and Unitel.

Context

With the enactment of the law, companies such as Sonangol and Unitel had to adapt to new regulatory requirements to ensure the protection of their users' personal data, establishing an important legal framework in a context where data protection was still developing.

Challenges

Operators faced notable difficulties, including:

- Implementation of Consent Systems: The need to develop proper systems to obtain consent from users was a critical issue, especially in an environment where privacy education was still in its early stages.

- Information Security: Protecting stored information has become a priority, requiring investments in technology and training to mitigate security risks.

Solution

Sonangol and Unitel have taken proactive measures to comply with the legislation:

1. Team Training: Both companies have invested significantly in training their teams on the new legislation, highlighting the importance of compliance at all levels of the organization.

2. Implementation of Security Technologies: Operators have adopted advanced security technologies, such as encryption and firewalls, to protect consumer data, as well as establishing a DPO to oversee these practices.

3. Clear Communication with Customers: Unitel has developed a clear communication strategy with its customers, informing them of its privacy practices and ensuring that users understand how their data is handled.

Results

Commitment to legal compliance has led to:

- Positive Reputation: Both companies have enjoyed a positive reputation in the market, reflected in increased consumer confidence and customer satisfaction.

- Avoid Legal Sanctions: Proactivity in complying with legislation has helped to avoid possible legal sanctions and strengthen the competitive position of operators in the Angolan market.

Chapter Summary

This chapter presented a detailed analysis of four practical cases that demonstrate how telecommunications companies are adapting to different data protection laws around the world.

Each case illustrates not only the challenges faced, but also the solutions implemented and the results obtained.

These examples underscore the importance of a proactive approach to compliance with data protection legislation, which not only ensures the safety of consumers but can also result in significant benefits for businesses, such as strengthening consumer trust, improving reputation, and increasing overall satisfaction.

Thus, the commitment to data protection proves to be not only a legal obligation, but also a strategic opportunity for telecommunications operators to stand out in a competitive and rapidly evolving market.

Conclusion: The Integration Between Data Protection and Telecommunications Expansion

The closing of this book invites us to reflect on the profound transformations that telecommunications have been undergoing in recent decades and the complexities that arise when we associate these changes with the universe of data protection.

Throughout the chapters, we seek to build an understanding of the dynamics that shape this expanding area, highlighting not only technological advances and their implications, but also the central role of data regulation, which is increasingly indispensable for the sustainability and security of digital development.

The Central Role of Telecommunications in the 21st Century

The advent of technologies such as 5G, the Internet of Things (IoT), and artificial intelligence is turning telecommunications into a driving force for modern society.

These innovations are opening up new opportunities for both business and everyday life, providing greater connectivity, efficiency, and new models of interaction with the digital world.

However, this exponential growth carries a huge responsibility, since the increase in connectivity directly implies an increase in the collection, storage and use of personal data.

In this way, as we advance technologically, concerns about data security and privacy also intensify.

The growth of telecommunications networks, therefore, cannot be discussed in isolation: it is imperative to integrate data protection as a fundamental basis for responsible and ethical development.

Topics Addressed: Challenges and Solutions

In previous chapters, we have explored the relationship between the expansion of telecommunications and data protection regulations from a variety of angles, addressing the complex challenges and opportunities that arise from this intersection. Below is a summary of the main themes that were deepened:

DATA PROTECTION AND SECURITY IN THE TELECOMMUNICATIONS SECTOR
CHALLENGES AND SOLUTIONS IN THE DIGITAL AGE

1. Global Connectivity and Data Exposure: We discussed how the evolution of telecommunications is increasing global interconnectivity while exposing users to a scenario where data is generated and shared at unprecedented levels.

Technologies such as 5G and IoT intensify this exposure, and with it, questions emerge about how to properly protect this information in large-scale networks.

2. Data Protection Regulations: The book outlined the importance of data protection regulations, such as the GDPR (General Data Protection Regulation of the European Union) and the LGPD (General Data Protection Law of Brazil).

Not only do they create a regulatory framework for privacy, but they also establish fundamental rights for users, such as the right to be forgotten, explicit consent, and data portability.

At the same time, we challenge the idea that regulation can be an obstacle to innovation, showing that it can instead encourage more responsible and innovative practices.

3. Public-Private Partnerships: We explore in detail the vital role of government-private sector partnerships. These collaborations are essential to ensure that the expansion of telecommunications networks is conducted responsibly, safely and in accordance with current legislation.

We discussed the importance of ongoing dialogue, creating global standards, and joint investments in cybersecurity to protect critical infrastructure and ensure consumer trust.

4. Responsible Innovation and Privacy by Design: One of the main concepts discussed was that of privacy by design, which consists of integrating data protection from the early stages of the development of new products and services.

This is a clear example of how data protection and innovation can go hand in hand, allowing companies and developers to adopt responsible practices while continuing to create and launch new technologies.

5. The Future of Telecommunications: Finally, we look at how telecommunications will continue to evolve in the coming decades, considering the impending advancements and their implications.

Smart cities, self-driving cars, and telemedicine are just a few examples of areas that rely heavily on telecommunications and consequently demand an increasingly robust approach to data protection.

Personal and Professional Application: Opportunities and Responsibilities

For readers, the reflections and analyses contained in this book offer not only a comprehensive overview of the current telecommunications and data protection landscape, but also practical guidance on how to successfully navigate this new environment. Both on a personal and professional level, there are numerous lessons to be drawn.

Professional Application

From a professional perspective, it is essential that leaders, managers, and technology professionals understand the need to integrate data protection practices into all phases of their projects.

Companies that can balance innovation with security will stay ahead of the competition, earning consumer trust and avoiding severe fines associated with privacy violations.

Professionals from all areas – not just technicians – should familiarize themselves with data protection legislation, as digital privacy has become a cross-cutting theme in several sectors, such as health, finance, education, and commerce.

Readers can also identify opportunities for growth and expertise. Information security, compliance with data regulations, and the development of privacy-by-design-based technologies are areas of enormous demand, with growing opportunities for those who have expertise in these fields.

Personal Application

On a personal level, reading this book serves as a reminder of the importance of protecting one's own data and understanding privacy rights. In a hyper-connected world, we are all constantly providing data, often without full awareness of how it is being used.

The book highlighted the need to be more critical and conscious about the permissions we grant, the privacy policies we accept, and the platforms on which we share our information.

In addition, the theme of digital literacy is central: as more connected devices enter our lives – from smartphones to smart home appliances – we need to be aware of cyber risks and the steps we can take to protect our data.

Tools such as encryption, two-factor authentication, and the use of VPNs are practices that can significantly improve the digital security of the average user.

The Future of Telecommunications and Data Protection

As we move towards an increasingly digital future, it is clear that telecommunications cannot be decoupled from data protection.

The challenge we face is to build a digital ecosystem that promotes technological progress while respecting the fundamental rights of privacy and protection of personal information.

The discussions developed here point to a future of continuous collaboration between governments, businesses and consumers, where everyone has a role to play.

Creating a secure and inclusive digital environment depends on both adopting responsible technological innovations and strictly adhering to data protection regulations.

Ultimately, the integration between technological growth and ethical responsibility outlines the path to the future of telecommunications.

This book sought to provide a deep understanding of this interconnectedness, allowing the reader not only to appreciate the challenges and opportunities, but also to be prepared to position themselves, whether in the personal or professional field, as an active and informed agent in the midst of the ongoing digital transformation.

Final Thoughts

This book is not just an analysis of telecommunications and data protection, but a call to action for all of us. The digital age is redefining the way we live, work, and interact, and it's up to us to ensure that this transformation is guided by the principles of ethics, responsible innovation, and respect for individual rights.

Readers are invited to apply the knowledge gained to improve their own practices, whether personal or professional, and to adopt a more active stance in building a digital future that is safe, inclusive and beneficial for all.

www.ingramcontent.com/pod-product-compliance
Lightning Source LLC
Chambersburg PA
CBHW062118220526
45471CB00010B/3784